YES,
I DO
&
I DID IT

Nadine Nelen

Copyright © 2014 by NNI PTY LTD

All rights reserved.

Cover design by NNI PTY LTD
Book design by NNI PTY LTD

Photography by Andrea Sproxton

No part of this book may be reproduced in any form or by any electronic or mechanical means including information storage and retrieval systems, without permission in writing from the author. The only exception is by a reviewer, who may quote short excerpts in a review.

Disclaimer

The author does not dispense medical, psychological or financial advice or prescribe the use of any technique as a form of treatment for physical, emotional, or medical problems without the advice of a physician, either directly or indirectly. The intent of the author is only to offer information of a general nature to help you in your quest for emotional and spiritual well-being. In the event you use any of the information the author and NNI PTY LTD assume no responsibility for your actions.

NNI PTY LTD books are available for order
through Ingram Press Catalogues

The names and significant details have been changed to protect the privacy of those whose generosity and good humor
have enriched my life.

Nadine Nelen

Visit my website at www.nadinenelen.com

Printed in the Australia, the U.S and Europe

First Printing: May 2014

First Printing 2014
By
Sojourn Publishing, LLC

NNI PTY LTD

ISBN 978-1-62747-051-3
Ebook ISBN 978-1-62747-052-0

To my Mum

Table of Contents

Leaving Home 2
Going Home 3
What Happened Before 5
Early Days 8
Growing Up 11
School 14
Writing 16
Bad Things Happen 17
First Travel 19
Growing Pains 21
Teenage Years 24
Beginning of the Search for Meaning 26
Artist or Not? 29
First Love 31
Continuing the Search for Meaning 33
More School 36
Daily Life—Early Days 37
Jobs 39
Family—We All Have One 41
Losses 43
Life Goes On 44
More Change 45
Getting it Back Together—Sorting Things Out 48
An Old Thought System to Believe and Teach 50
The Wish List 55
Aussie, Aussie, Aussie, OI OI OI 57

Working in Australia 60
Moving to the Seaside 65
My Own Boss Again 71
Dating in Australia 77
Lessons in Love 85
Things That Make My Day 89
Reprogramming 91
Some Other Things I Noticed 92
Allow 95
Money and Love 97
Feelings 98
The Body 99
The Mind 103
Change and Time 105
Changing 108
Balance 112
Acknowledgments 117

Usually, stories start with once upon a time. Mine starts from before I experienced time as I do now by living in a body. I have memories that bring me way back. They are like little tapes that I can play in my head. I can feel the movies as if they are happening in the present moment. These tapes are from before I was in this body. Sometimes I was in another body, and sometimes it was an astral body, a bundle of energy without the heaviness I have here on earth. In one of these movie tapes, I remember vividly how I had a spiritual guide who came and saw me about making some more progress by returning back to earth, also referred to as "school." I was not too keen to begin with, as I enjoyed being in this other realm where my dreams were materialised immediately, and I was not pulled back with the heavy energy that goes with having a body and space and time and all the other paradigms that would come along with that. Anyway, I did want to make progress and I knew there was something I needed to do to get back to a state of oneness. I had promises to fulfil and tangos to dance. A gathering happened with other souls and, in a nonverbal way, we decided on what would be best for each of us to learn our lessons. Lessons to bring us back to love. In the state where all is one with love and all is forgiven. Back to our original state of being before we fell asleep and forgot that we were part of all that is.

LEAVING HOME

I see letters, words. A story is forming from before I was born: how I would flow in and out of my body, hearing my parents argue, and looking forward to join with them. I was in a place with lots of light, laughter, and love. The opposite of where I was going. I thought that if I join the darkness I could make them feel better. I can bring my little light into this darkness and bravely shine some light on it all. They will be happy to see me and will rejoice in having light in their life. I will be welcomed with open arms. So I started packing my bags. Joking. In that realm, I travelled light and started my descent into duality, the world. It was like falling asleep. Suddenly, everything became dark and heavy—as if someone had turned off the lights and, instead of air, there was mud encompassing me. I had difficulty breathing until somebody smacked me on the bum. I could suddenly scream! Yeah! Here I am the light of your life!

It was cold, wet and dark. I felt a rough towel, and the midwife said: "It is a girl with all toes and fingers and no visible handicaps; I will let her come into this life. You know I never delivered a disabled child."

Lucky me I had no disability, or my descent into the world would have been brief.

"We will put her away now so you can rest."

My first night on earth, I slept alone. I was still cold but dry now and in a pram with little ducks. Then the lights went out, and I was covered in darkness.

I quickly went back home and felt immediately encompassed by the light. My Mentor was there, and he assured me I could do this. *"You have to remember, you didn't want an easy life. This is what you chose in order to bring out the best in you. If it would be any easier, you wouldn't learn and grow. You can do this. I promise you I will always be there in your darkest moments just call out my name. I am always there for you. Now go back and be happy."*

After that I seldom could go back home. I mostly stayed in the material world and got really sucked in deeply. I fell asleep big time. Every day, little by little, my mind filled itself with the beliefs of the people around me, until they were my own. I believed everything they told me, everything they did, and really tried to be there for them. After two years, I just knew this is it! I have lost contact with reality, and I am now fully conditioned in the dream. No way back. Or is there?

GOING HOME

I was taken home. It was a very cold spring. We had twenty centimetres of snow and I loved to watch the flakes come down. What I did not like was my parents arguing all the time. They were discussing the fact that I was conceived at a time when they were not having sex, although they did not use that word, of course. It was clear what the argument was about. My mother felt very guilty; she knew who my biological father was. Mr. War, a business acquaintance of my father, was visiting us often and they just followed some urge. It was never meant to be nor to last, let at all give any result.

Once she knew she was pregnant, she went to the doctor panicking and saying, "I don't want this child." My mother was seven months pregnant, too late to get rid of me, and it was illegal in Belgium anyway. I felt in the water in the womb that I was being rejected and it made me feel very itchy. Who wants to be confronted with a product of their extramarital activities? The dust settled and, to punish herself, she made my father sell his business and take on a steady job again. The sale went pear-shaped and they lost all their money. From there on, she was very scared of losing all.

I remember that summer seeing Mr. War standing at our gate. I could feel some emotion welling up in him, and then he turned around and walked away. Why? He knew he was my father. I knew he was my father. Just that deep knowledge, gut feeling, where you know there is no room for mistakes. I wanted him to stay, but he had closed the gate, walked away, and never looked back.

For a while, I kept hoping to see him again and, I did. But it was just a very short visit. It must have been very difficult for him to walk away like that, but, in his belief system, it was the only option he had. I stared and stared, wishing him back, but to no avail. From then on, the husband of my mother became my father.

I don't think any of them realised how I experienced all this in a conscious way. This was the start of a belief I held for a long time. The belief that love walks away, and that strong men are afraid of showing emotions. For the first time, I felt really deserted and alone, not loved. I was convinced I was not lovable because I was not good enough. How is anybody going to love me if even my own maker can't stay around?

WHAT HAPPENED BEFORE

Meanwhile, my mother turned into stone. I guess the guilt was devouring her so much that she also experienced the feeling of not being good enough, but in a huge way. She was raised in a very dysfunctional family.

Her father had two wives, and my grandmother found this out on his deathbed. After struggling with lung cancer for over a year, he knew his time was up, so he asked my grandmother to line up his children. She put them all in front of him, and then he said, "No, not these ones. I also want to see the other ones once more before I die." She thought he was hallucinating from the heavy painkillers he was given, but he was persistent. "I want to see my 'other' children." He gave more details, but my grandmother refused to contact them. He was not married to the other woman, so I guess she had no legal claim, and I think the kids had another name. I always wondered who "my other" family was, and if they knew about this story as well.

My mother was a teenager during the war and had a good friend who died in the bombing of a movie theatre in Antwerp. She told the story to me, how people were being taken out of a house in their street after a V1 bomb fell on it, and they were only fifty centimetres long and all black like a piece of coal. Then there were the German soldiers who would come every day into the bakery and ordered to take away all the bread for the army. One of the Gestapo guys was writing letters to her, and she was very scared of him.

The neighbour was betraying a lot of people to get extras. So one day, he betrayed my grandfather for hiding an English soldier. Grandpa was sleeping in bed when they came into the house to search everywhere, but they couldn't find any English parachutist. The landing of the soldier and receiving of help and civilian clothes had happened in the domain my grandfather used for hunting. He gave his parachute to my grandfather who turned it into a wedding dress for his oldest daughter who had a shotgun wedding, because she had to hurry up before "the bun in the oven" started showing.

Life just continued during the war. There was still love and sex and also hate and envy, and people trying to survive by betraying other people. It was all part of the game. One of the stories that horrified me as a kid was about my great uncle who was so hungry he had killed his dog, a German shepherd. He was frying it on a spit, and the German soldiers walked by. He told him it was a sheep, and he received some good money for it and coupons to buy food. At least he didn't have to eat his dog, and the "bad guys" were happy too, as they rarely had good meat during the war.

Years after the war, my grandfather got upset with a friend of his who was bragging a lot about how good his knowledge of eating "wild" animals was. He invited him to eat "rable," a special dish made from the back of a hare and very rare to find. He had no time to go hunting days before the dinner, so at the last minute, he got the cat and put her (dead of course) in the wine with garlic and spices overnight. Next day, the "friend" came for dinner, and, while eating, he was praising the quality of the hare and boasting what a connoisseur he was. Upon finishing the meal, my grandfather said, "Jeff, I am sorry. But actually we ate the cat. I had no time to go hunting and, as you can see, this type of bone is typical for a cat, not a wild animal like a hare. One has square bones and the other has more rounded ones." Jeff never ran that fast to empty his stomach, while my grandfather was laughing his head off and had no issues at all eating his own cat.

My other grandparents were a weird couple, too. My paternal grandfather was fifteen years or so older than my grandmother, and she never ever grew up. He must have loved her to bits and spoiled her all the time. She was the spitting image of Mrs. Bucket in *Keeping up Appearances*. He died young in his sixties from a heart attack, and she had no idea how to live without him. In her late fifties, she had to go and live permanently in an old people's home. Even though she had no real illness or health problems, she didn't last very long in that awful place. Ten years later she died. I used to call the cause of her dying "self-inflicted old age" because she believed she was old and therefor sick and close to death. Her health was ok and she could have lived much longer if she wouldn't have convinced herself otherwise. She was emotionally detached and very severe with my father. She never let him be his playful self. Everyone had to pretend and keep up appearances of being a highly sophisticated, happy family. Formal clothes had to be worn most of the time, and new ones were bought as often as possible so they could take family pictures in them. They had three kids, and my father was the middle one. He often complained about his mother and how she had become a financial burden for him in her older years. He said, "I swear I will never do that to my kids. I do not want them to pay for me." He is in his eighties and still lives with his partner in a townhouse and has never asked us for any help.

EARLY DAYS

In church, I had memories of times long gone, and I just stood there. I refused to sit down while trying to connect with God. *Who can connect to God sitting down?* I thought. We rise and shine in his image. I always made a cross with my left hand, and my father named me The Orthodox, like the Russians. The statues in the church intrigued me, and I used to draw them in my father's notebook. I was always making drawings, and no pen or paper was safe around me.

I was often told the story that, when I was a little baby, I made my first drawing on a piece of carton while they were changing my diapers. The pencil was stuck between my toes, and people enjoyed how I would make drawings with my toes. I even smuggled pens in bed so I could write on the wall. I had severe eczema, so my hands were tied to the bedpost to avoid scratching myself. Luckily, I could draw with my feet on the angled ceiling above my bed.

My sister often had to explain in school why the moon and Saint Nicholas and his boat were on her report card. Lots of official documents had the same drawings over and over again: the man with the long white beard holding a golden sceptre and standing on the boat that came straight from Spain. Maybe I had an early way of making vision boards. I did end up working as a shipping agent and going on board many ships. The holy man stood for what I knew to be good and spiritual in my early days. He seemed abundant to me, because of his golden sceptre and the big bishop rings he had on his fingers. He came from overseas, and I was always drawn to travelling and going overseas. Although I ended up travelling a lot, it was mostly in airplanes. I am not fond of travelling over the water as the motion sickness often sticks up its ugly head.

The moon and sun were two other favourites of mine and had to be drawn on every surface that would allow it. I adored both and would follow the moon at night from the back of our car. I was amazed how it would always follow me home. It made me feel blessed.

My father calling me an Orthodox in church because of my Russian behaviour made sense thirty years later when, in regression, I saw myself in a past life as a man of the church. I had this long beard and very angry face. I was a main driver of a split in the Orthodox Church and had a big fight with my best friend over it. I took a heavy candelabra smashed his skull in.

I still carried that guilt of killing my best friend over a religious argument, and I still, for the same reason, dislike organised religions. Even only yesterday, I was asked if I was Russian. It is amazing how we can carry through characteristics from past lives into the next one.

After I had the regression, I had serious doubts that what I had just experienced was merely a nightmare or more. So I looked up the Orthodox Church and the year I thought my past life took place, and it explained that there was a big split in that religion. Two different opinions had to split ways. It suddenly all made a lot of sense, and, at the same time, it was scary to realise these things make sense.

It is easier in the beginning—when we try to awaken to the spiritual side we have inside us—to ignore it and see things as a coincidence and forget them as soon as we experienced them: freak stuff from nature. To keep on living with them as a part of my daily reality took a lot of courage and getting over myself. I was so self-conscious about what others would think about me when I would say, "Guess what? In my past life I had this same experience, and that is how I handled it. So now I want to handle it differently." They would for sure laugh at me and call me crazy, a lunatic with lots of imagination and fantasy stuff happening in her head.

But after lots and lots of serendipities, regressions, and messages from deceased people, there comes a day when one has to admit it is part of their reality, just as the sun and the moon. I mean I can't explain how the radio waves travel through the air, but I know how to get music out of a radio. It is the same with the Reiki I practice or other healings that I see happening. I can't explain it, but I can see the result. I improved my eyesight with EFT, short for Emotional Freedom Techniques. A technique that consists of tapping with two fingers meridian points on the body while saying affirmations. I don't know how it works, but it did in my case.

GROWING UP

I had a sister nine years my senior, and for her I was a living doll. She loved taking care of me. When she arrived back from school, she used to look after me. We still had the business and, during the day, I was left mostly to myself in the back of the garden. An old uncle used to check on me and yell to my mother, "Germaine, she is wet again!" and then change my diapers. Both my parents were way too busy to spend time with me.

I also had the cats keeping me company, and I imitated their behaviour. I made similar noises when I cried. I learned to walk by myself in a walker, but one day, it tumbled over and I came into the kitchen on all fours carrying a dead mouse in my mouth. I had not only adopted beliefs but also the behaviour that I saw around me.

My world became harsher every day and when we moved to the new house it became even more tense. My father worked crazy hours to avoid being at home in this tension. For a sensitive man, it must have been hell to wake up and go to sleep in it every day. Day after day, like in *Groundhog Day*, the same thing happens over and over again. My mother was stressed to the max and kept telling me, "don't attach yourself to anything, because tomorrow the bailiff will come and take it all away from you. The only thing he will leave will be a chair, a table, and a bed. Nothing else."

My imagination worked overtime, and I could just see the bailiff taking it and how I would have to live sharing the three items with my family. I was hoping he left me with some pens and paper…I needed them to be able to draw. My mother seemed to blame my father for the wrong things that happened in her life. I translated this belief that you only got in trouble by not being clever enough. It was, therefore, very important to be highly intelligent and clever. That was the only way to stay out of trouble and have a happy life. I kept repeating this belief many times. I would never trust anyone—not even myself—to take the right decisions and to take care of me. I became specialised in beating myself over the head each time I made the slightest mistake.

It seemed also important that when I grew up, I had to be self-reliant and never ever get married or be dependant on a man. My mother had no car, no driver's license and no income. She felt a victim of the situation. I believed a lot of things she said and, at the same time, I tried to make her see certain things positively in this world. Because she was no longer working, she had nothing to do all day but to think about what can go wrong, and she was an expert in it. She could turn anything around in no time and make it something awful. She possessed the opposite of the touch of Midas; instead of gold, everything turned into shit. Her days were spent leaning on our kitchen counter, staring out of the window onto the street, and making up stories. She went to the shops on her bike and had very few friends. Some friends were hilarious, as they lived on the border of the society with probably an IQ of 90 or less. Maria from the chicken farm was one like that. She looked like Andre Van Duin, a Dutch comedian known for the role of a stupid bloke he used to play. I never understood why mother would have her over for tea; she smelled bad, probably like chicken manure with cauliflower mixed in it. She talked weird and had the strangest stories.

One day, it was decided we would get chickens too. After three weeks, they were still not laying eggs, and we had no idea what was wrong with them. Maria was asked for her expert advice. She took every single chicken up her lap and put her finger in their bum before smelling her finger. She said, "Give them another ten days, and they will start laying eggs. All of them!" She was spot on! Because they had no phone, Maria's family would also visit us to make phone calls. Her daughter Astrid, who was a good athlete, would walk in with a piece of paper and a telephone number on it. I was about five or six, and Astrid would have been seventeen. She would hand me the piece of paper and ask me to dial the number. They considered me the technical expert, and I loved the phone and making phone calls. Once I heard the phone was ringing on the other side, I would hand over the receiver to her (we had a black phone made of heavy material before they used plastic). She would wait until the other side answered and shout very loudly: "Hi, it is me! I ran, I won!" And she would hang up, give me a coin, and leave. Just like Julius Caesar, "veni vidi vici"!

SCHOOL

I remember staring outside as well and wishing to be able to join the neigbourhood kids going to school. I had enough of being locked in this house with a depressed mother and with no means to make her feel better. If I could only go to school and become clever, then I would be able to help her.

And then one day—yes, I was only two and a half and allowed in early—I got ready for my first school day. I was so excited I did not sleep the night before. When we arrived in the classroom, I noticed a lot of kids were crying, and it got to me. Why were they doing this? We finally made it here, and then they were sad? That made no sense to me at all. After one hour listening to them wailing, I got up on my chair and yelled: "Shut up! You are giving me a headache!"

The teacher almost wet herself laughing. Never ever had she seen anything like that on a first day. Best part was that they were all terrified, and not one of them dared to cry after that.

Was I a born bully? I hope to think not, but I couldn't understand them and made my frustration known loud and clear. I wanted to accumulate knowledge so I could help my family to be happy and to find my way back to happiness, and they were just wailing? It was not received very well, and my first steps of being less honest about expressing my feelings were made. I learned to not stand out and try to fit in more; not to hurt others with being honest about what I was really thinking.

One day, we were allowed to paint on the windows. It was amazing. I loved it! The next day, all the parents came to our classroom to look at the paintings, and I heard people saying, "This is nice. Surely, the kid did not do this by herself; the teacher must have been helping her big time."

My father became upset and said to them: "You have no idea how talented my daughter is in painting, and she did this all by herself. Only the other day, she made a portrait of me, and it bares an amazing resemblance." A bit exaggerated, of course, but one of the nicest things I remember him doing for me. I had the gift of being able to make very realistic drawings as a very young child, and some grown-ups found that hard to believe.

WRITING

The next thing that intrigued me was the act of writing—putting thoughts on paper. My sister would sit at her desk and write her homework. She didn't seem to enjoy it, but I thought it was amazing, because it was like drawing but communicated even more clearly what you wanted to say.

She gave in to my endless nagging and taught me how to read and write by the age of five. I read lots and lots of books and loved it. It took me into another world, and I forgot all about the problems and strife at home. Some pink books my sister had were about doctors falling in love with poor nurses, and they seemed so much more romantic than what I had seen so far at home.

I had found romantic novels from my grandmother and enjoyed the sugary sweet horrendous stories about poor orphans getting suddenly rich. I daydreamed that I was an orphan, and that my real parents would come and take me home to their castle. I did not feel at home at all where I was and needed to escape. The escape came with the writers, so I read everything I could find in the house.

One day, there was nothing left to read for me, so I asked my father if I could go to the library and borrow some books. "No," he said, "you are too young. I want you to wait until you are seven."

I was devastated. I needed to quickly get more knowledge and also more ways to escape at the same time. So every Sunday, I kept two franks in my pocket, franks I was supposed to give to the church, and I went to the library at the entrance of the church. I thought that God would be okay if I spent it there, as it was still his library. The parish clerk betrayed me. He said, "Mark, do you realise your daughter only gives one frank, not two, for the last collection? Are times that bad?" I got accused of not only being heretic but also of stealing goods from the church and therefore from God. Luckily, I was too young to go to confession.

BAD THINGS HAPPEN

I did not get banished from the church, as I remember doing my holy communion all in white and finally with long hair. I used to have short hair like a boy, and some people thought I was a boy because of my deep voice. I played the postman most of the time and loved it. It was nice to be in white and hoping I would go back to the state I was in before I fell asleep, a time when I was close to the light where I came from. I knew something was going to happen, but what? Three months later, I was riding my push-bike with a girlfriend, and we saw a car parked on the way. The man got out and lured me into the woods. My friend was clever, and she peddled straight home.

He was up to no good, of course. When I started to realise he was playing dirty games with me and wanted to take me even deeper in the woods, I got scared so I ran and ran.

The brother of another friend brought me home after I arrived at their place with torn clothes and very distressed. They noted down the license plate of the car that was still around and gave it to my mother. She called the police and they said, "Sorry, ma'am, we are a bit too busy at the moment. So if you could call back later, that would be nice." She put me in bed. In the middle of the night, I woke up and my father was in my room. He got home from work and was raving on about taking me to the police. Oh my God, I thought I did something wrong here. I should have driven off with Lisa, my friend, while I could, instead of wanting the attention of this grown man. For a while, I felt really interesting and grown-up while this older man was touching me, but part of me knew this was very wrong and not supposed to happen. Why did he remove my underwear and what were these other games he was talking about that he wanted to play? I was torn between staying and being like a grown-up, or to running away and staying an innocent child.

My father lifted me out of bed and we drove to the police. I was terrified.

We arrived in the dark and I had to go to the toilet. The policeman on duty pointed to the back and said, "Just go there and then to the left." I was confused and went to the right and saw the jail cells. What if they will lock me up here? I'd better shut up now and never ever say anything again about this whole mess that I created with my curiosity.

I went back after finding the real toilets and did not speak about it again. They said, "She might be too tired to talk about it, so tomorrow we will come to your place to take a statement."

They arrived the next morning, and I was in agony. But I kept saying, "I don't remember, I don't remember, I don't know anything!" I was so embarrassed. Finally, they left and left me alone.

FIRST TRAVEL

I continued to live my life. We went on a trip to Spain and I loved it: the warm climate, the different smells and foods, the other languages. I always loved languages, and I would stand in front of a mirror pretending to give speeches in other languages. I would make it sound similar to English or French. When I was in Spain, I picked up Spanish in no time. The whole trip was so great that I hoped we would go back every year. But we never did.

My mother had decided that travelling was not her thing, and that she preferred to stay home. She used to say: "I would be at my happiest when I would live all alone by myself in a hut in the middle of a huge forest". She must have loved her solitude more than anything else. I sometimes feel like that too. I can be alone for days and not miss human company. I get into another space and just enjoy the creativity that can flow out of me. I retract into my inner sanctuary and try to stay in the moment.

My father, on the other hand, was more of an extrovert and was driving around all day as a sales man. He had a big shiny Mercedes that my mother cleaned every day, and he was very proud of it. After normal working hours, he would go and paint houses to make sure we had enough money. I think he was still paying off some debt. I was not kept in the loop of the exact situation, but the only thing I sometimes wished for was to have new toys. My mother did not believe in toys and saw them as a waste of money. If you want something, go and make it yourself. I got access to our garage and my father's working bench and loved to make stuff there. A movie theatre out of an old shoe box, with a piece of paper in the back covered with my drawings that could be rolled over two sticks so it would look like a movie being shown. A miniature house and things that were not really the toys I wanted but kind of looked alike with a lot of imagination.

My sister and I were growing more apart as she started dating, and I was teasing her a lot. I never understood her motives in those days. She seemed happy being a dressmaker and just sitting at home on the couch, not doing anything in particular. She married her first or second boyfriend and had children. I could not imagine a life like that. I would rather be dead. I wanted to travel and learn lots of things—see the world and get out there like they do in books.

My heroes were writers of books, not so much the actors or musicians, although I did have a poster of

David Cassidy and one of Robert Redford on the wall in my room. Writers held more attraction to me. I would fall in love with another writer every year and fall asleep with his book in my arms staring at his picture. Every night, with the little bedside table lamp on, I would stay up late to read until I fell asleep. Most mornings I woke up with the light still on. I was still afraid of the dark and preferred to sleep with the lights on. I started to feel sad about the discrepancy between the life in my dreams and the reality. When I was not escaping in some novel, I realised things were not looking anywhere near what I thought they should.

GROWING PAINS

My parents still argued a lot, and I just didn't understand why I was not able to help them more. What could I do? They were the grown-ups. Why did they keep themselves in this prison of their own choice? They could split up and do something they enjoyed? So I became alienated more and more from them.

At school, I was having problems fitting in. No one could read nor write in the first class, and I thought they were all mentally disabled. I didn't understand that seven-year-old kids couldn't read and write. The teachers were just following the traditional program and to me that was very boring since I knew most of what they were talking about. I looked for distractions to make these long days bearable. Consequently I received remarks on my report card saying things like: "Nadine is stubborn and not easy in the class. She doesn't seem to understand that we can't do things her way". They tried putting tape on mouth to prevent me from speaking. They tied the strings of my apron to the back of my chair to prevent me from walking around. I had to stand in the corner a lot to meditate about my sins. I did not warm to the nuns; luckily, there were only a few of them. They seemed very unchristian and harsh to me, not at all how I imagined a "bride of Jesus" should be like. They used their white wedding band to beat me around the head with, not to pray or be nice and forgiving.

I haggled a lot and exchanged things, trading them in and preferably up. I think I came home one day with a golden watch, which, of course, I had to give back as soon as my mother found out.

I had lots of nosebleeds in those days and, one day, it just didn't stop bleeding. I had to hang over the bathtub and tried everything, but nothing seemed to stop the bleeding. After six hours, I was still bleeding. My father came home and got upset with my mother for nearly having me bleed to dead. They grabbed me and took off in his new Mercedes to the hospital. I always got car sick as a child and, because they had not given me medication beforehand against motion sickness, I started to feel very queasy. I had not eaten any food since breakfast, so my stomach was basically filled with blood. Next thing I knew, it squirted out and straight on to the white leather looking roof inside my father's car, covering the whole interior and all the passengers. My parents arrived in the hospital carrying me, and we are all covered in blood, as if we had all been in a horrendous car crash. Needless to say, they put me immediately on a stretcher. When they asked what had happened and if everyone was okay, they suddenly understood it was blood from my stomach and everything slowed down.

"Oh, I see, it is only a nosebleed. We will get a doctor for you," the nurse said.

When I finally got to the doctor, he made me sit up straight, which was very difficult because I felt so weak and wanted to lie down. He said, "I now have to burn the inside of your nose, so you will have to hold this tray under your nose and don't move. The iron is hot, and I don't want to hurt you."

I was terrified. The burning was fierce, and I almost dropped the tray. He got very upset with me and said, "Try that one more time and you will cop it."

What an angry man. He must have been very tired after too many long days. I was the one at the receiving end of his frustrations. We made it back home. After that, the nose bleedings were stopped with burning drops, and eventually they stopped altogether. I looked up "nose bleedings" the other day in Louise Hay's book, and it said: "A need for recognition. Feeling unrecognized and unnoticed. Crying for love." The affirmations she recommends is: "I love and approve of myself. I recognize my own true worth. I am wonderful."

And that is what I was trying to do: get attention, get recognition. I tried to do my best all the time and just didn't understand why my parents didn't love me and didn't love each other. It made no sense to live like that. I would rather be dead than have a frustrating loveless life like that. But they continued as they were taught based on their own limiting beliefs from their young days.

TEENAGE YEARS

The teenage years for me, although nothing out of the ordinary happened, were like the dark ages. They seemed to crawl by in a boring way, and they were dark with no hope in sight. Everywhere I looked, I had to oblige and do things that I would rather not do. I did not know how to escape this. The things I wanted to do were either not allowed or I could not afford them. I had adopted the idea "there never is enough" very well and practised it daily, creating as much scarcity as I could. When I was thirteen years old, I had to go and work in a cigar factory during school holidays. I hated it. I had to get up early at the crack of dawn and ride 25 km on my bike all the way to this factory.

The place smelled awful, and the women who worked there were so unlike anything I knew that they could have been aliens from another planet. My father said it was good for me to know and experience what kind of work people who did not have an education have to do to earn a dollar. It was awful. I went every day, and there was no way I wasn't going to go. The money came in handy to buy clothes, cigarettes, and books. The women never accepted me, as I was a rare bird to them as well. I was studying Latin while they could hardly read, let alone write. When they got a letter from the management of the factory, they came to see me. I had to read it out loud and explain what the meaning was. They asked if they should become a member of the union to defend their rights or just ignore the letters from management. They had difficulties grasping concepts and saw anyone with a nice car or wealthy assets as an enemy. Rich people were bad, and good people were poor, just like them. They were happy to sing all day to the same music recorded on tapes played over and over again while packing box after box of cigars, and then at four run—like their life depended on it—to the bus to get home to make dinner for the husband and kids. Some were badly treated by their husbands, especially after payday when their sweetheart had a couple too many drinks. His hands would get loose, and it was usually the wife who bore the consequences. I sat across the table from a seventeen-year-old who had five kids and regularly showed up at work with a black eye. I could not imagine what that would be like. She got pregnant at twelve and got married in the same dress in which she did her Holy Communion a couple of months before. I swore I would not end up like that. No marriage and no babies until l had lived my life. Even though it was a hard lesson, it was a useful one, and it taught me also to be self-reliant. What was not so good was that I started a pattern to have jobs that I hated but would say, "The money is a consolation, so I will continue doing this." There is no way for me to make a living and at the same time do something I enjoy doing. Another limiting belief was created in my mind.

BEGINNING OF THE SEARCH FOR MEANING

Around the age of ten, I started to have an interest in the Bible and other books that would hopefully give me answers to questions like: "Why was I here on earth?" and "Why am I going through these experiences?" I just didn't get the sense of it. Why was I born? According to my mother, to suffer. The Bible seemed to say the same. Even though Jesus had already suffered for my sins, that apparently wasn't enough. Do I have to suffer, too? It would be easier to get into heaven being poor than rich, and being poor was a form of suffering, being deprived. In heaven, that was all made up for, and we could eat as much rice pudding with a golden spoon as we wanted. I didn't like the dish so I never believed a word of that story. How could "being in heaven" be eating something awful? I had to read the Bible without telling our priest, because Catholics—as apposed to Lutherans—were not allowed to read the Bible by themselves. Only the priests could read it. They presumed we would not be able to make the right deduction from biblical texts, as we were not inaugurated, not schooled to understand the Bible. And now I think that was pure projection of the Catholic Church, as they were and are still not reading properly what it is saying. Being an institution, they have problems evolving with the world. The world has changed a lot, but they stick to the same worldview of hundreds of years ago, and then are amazed that they lose popularity. With the right marketing guy and social networking online, they might become popular again—if, of course, they change their worldview as well and referred more to some of their great theologians.

Anyway, that is not going to happen, and that is probably how it is supposed to be. Meanwhile, the pain from living in my world grew stronger, and I got a bit older. Around the age of fourteen, I started to drink alcohol to make it go away. It brought me a soft cloudy feeling, and I forgot all my worries. I went to café's during the day to drink beer, or I had some with friends when their parents were out. I was too young to be allowed out at night, but during the day, on non-school days, no one said anything. I had two friends, who both had a father with a drinking problem. One friend's father would go and have some beers after work and forget to come home in time for dinner. So we would have to drive around on our pushbikes, visiting all the pubs in the village to try to find him. We usually ended up having beers with him and we all got home drunk. I was only thirteen…maybe fourteen years old. The other friend's parents were divorced, and she lived with her father. He drank all day long. We had to hide the bottles of whisky in her underwear, so he would not find it and drink it all. He would often pass out and not remember anything the next day. For the first time, I heard the word "delirium." I even saw her father having a *delirium tremens*.

We didn't seem to mind on the outside, because we considered ourselves as tough as nails. On the inside, it was not the same. We saw the advantage of it all, as well as how much freedom this created for us. We told him stories that we would go and sleep at my parents' place, but then we stayed out all night to party. One night, he did go and check with my parents, and they were very worried the next day. I told them we were at his place the whole time, and that he was too far gone to notice we were sleeping in the camper trailer in the garden. We got away with it.

I picked up smoking, which was very difficult because I was afraid of fire and I had to use a lighter to light my cigarettes. It was absolutely forbidden, and that alone was reason enough to keep on going and to try not to get caught too much. I got into trouble in school about it, and, because I was a good student, they let me off the hook. My two friends could not follow me in the Latin-Greek classic studies, so they eventually left school and we lost contact. My parents seemed to have the rule that if you have good results in school, you are allowed to do whatever you want outside school. So I made sure my results were good however they were not good enough for my mother. She was very demanding. I would get 95 percent and she would say: "How can you be so stupid? If you get that much right, you had no reason to have some things wrong—unless you did something very stupid." It reinforced my belief that I was not good enough.

ARTIST OR NOT?

At seven years old, I started going to drawing school on Wednesday afternoons and loved it. For ten years, I was the number one, and then one year I came in second after Ignace Krekels. He was really happy not to be second all the time and continued later on to study at the Academia in Gent and be a full-time artist. I had upset the teacher by refusing to draw something in a certain style, and I had to pay the price. I also once won a nice prize with another drawing contest. It was organised by a company that sold kitchens.

They wanted us all to draw our present kitchen. Ours was in the middle of being renovated, so that is how I drew it. And because it was so different from all the other drawings, I guess, I won a gorgeous desk that served me very well for many years to come. I was over the moon to finally have my own desk to sit at and draw and write.

I did get the message loud and clear from everyone around me: drawing school was a hobby and in no way should I consider becoming an artist. Artists are poor people and they smell. They drink. They are unhappy and they cut their ear off.

I said, "But what about Rubens? He was rich and famous in his days, and he was an artist."

Answer: "In those days, things were different, and you are not exactly Rubens."

So I copied some of his drawings as good as I could, and indeed my style was very different. The teacher who taught oil painting said years later to me that I had the same style of using my space and brush as Rik Wouters. I was in heaven, but then I started thinking I would never be as good. He died at the age of thirty-four from pneumonia. He was so poor he could not afford heating or decent food. His paintings are now worth a fortune, but that happened after he died. So they told me that the only famous artists worth the money are dead, and when they were still alive, they were very hungry. "Even Van Gogh never sold a painting while he was alive," I was told. I lost most of my motivation to become a professional artist. It all seemed way too difficult, and I had enough stuff annoying me as it was.

I started to be interested in boys—and that was, of course, something different. I thought all my friends had experienced their first sexual acts, and I felt left behind. I thought I'd better get my act together and hurry up to belong. I knew I was not good enough, but at least I could try to fit in and talk as they did about sexual experiences. Little did I know they were just bragging, and when I found out they were still virgins, it was too late. Now I was the one who no longer fitted in, because I had experience and they didn't. It was not very pleasant, but I kept trying, hoping one day I might see the pleasure in it similar to smoking.

I was reading the Dutch scandal writers at night: Jan Cremer, Jan Wolkers, and Jef Geeraerts. They went on and on about sex, but it had nothing to do with the clumsy quickies my boyfriend and I had on the weekends. He was a sweet guy, but after a year or so I got bored so we broke it off. I didn't know what I really wanted. I only knew that was not it. I tried several ones, and nothing seemed to work out.

FIRST LOVE

Then one day, when I was seventeen, I fell in love. I really fell. He was at my school, and he had black hair and brown eyes. His name was Christophe. He seemed so mature, although he was only one year older. He drove a BMW motorbike to school, and I got to know him better on a school trip to Paris. We actually spent the night together on that trip, I think. He was an avid reader and introduced me to Nabokov. "Light of my life, fire of loins my sin my soul" (Lolita). I thought I finally found my soul mate and saw already how we would be happy in the future by reading books and going to jazz clubs. He gave me lots of books to read, and the speed-reader I am devoured two to three books a week. I was in heaven. After three months or so, he told me he wanted to break up with me. He broke my heart. For the first time, I knew what it felt like. I cried and cried and cried, but the only reason he gave me was that I read too fast. No way could I grasp the essence of literature by reading that fast, he proclaimed.

His best friend, George, saw my suffering and tried to cheer me up. He became my boyfriend for the next couple of years, as he was the closest thing to Christophe. But they saw less and less of each other, so I did not really get to stay close to Christophe. I loved the family of the new boyfriend. They had amazing

Sunday morning breakfasts with very interesting people at the table. My favourite guest on those breakfasts was Max Wildiers. I loved to listen to his stories. He was a Capuchin and had studied theology in Rome and biology in Belgium. He used to lecture in San Francisco at the university but was retired when I met him. He talked a lot about Teilhard de Chardin from whom he published the works without the Catholic Church prosecuting him. Max raved about Alfred N. Whitehead and the way he saw God, and how the Catholic Church should follow these worldviews. God is not some nasty old man up there in the sky, but actually a friend who understands.

It made all so much sense, and it opened up a whole new world. I was impressed by the knowledge Max had, not only of history, the war and other countries, but especially of languages. He spoke Latin fluently. At breakfast, we would usually speak English, as the stepfather of George—Jim—was from Philadelphia. Jim had a degree in philosophy and always provided great input during the conversations.

Jim was writing his own book about the creativity of the mind, which I typed out for him. I don't remember the exact content. I do remember that at that stage, he was not into God and spirituality. He was specialised in Hegel and existential phenomenology. Over the years, Jim became a specialist in the Course in Miracles and worked together with Kenneth Wapnick to have in translated into Dutch. He continued to write papers with explanations about the course, and I used to type them out for him.

CONTINUING THE SEARCH FOR MEANING

Jim was and is my spiritual mentor, and we keep in contact, even though I now live in another continent. When I consult Jim for advice, he turns inside and asks his guide—which he refers to as his boss—what he needs to tell me to help me on my path. He mostly taught me to trust my instincts and to follow what I feel as the right path deep down inside me. It has been a great service to me and helped me over many hurdles.

I Am That from Sri Nisargadatta is one of the first spiritual books I really became obsessed by, and also "Autobiography of a Yogi". I thought all Indians were highly spiritual beings, and that we in the West had lost our way. We do not know about the things they see as common daily knowledge. We are stuck in another belief system that takes us further away from the truth instead of bringing us closer. The essence of existence was my main concern. Why am I here? What is the purpose of life? Do we only have one life, or do we have many? The past lives that I seem to remember, are they real or do I make them up as I go? Like I do in this book.

To a teenager, there is not much sense in life. I had inherited the belief in scarcity from my mother, so I made sure I only dated guys with a certain status. George, when he turned eighteen, got hold of his inheritance, and suddenly we were rich; we could afford all kind of things that most young people could not. We went to a Renault garage and looked at a nice car. The car salesman did not take us very seriously, so George got a bit upset.

When we closed the deal, the guy asked, "So, how are you going to pay for this brand new car?"

George asked, "Do you want cash, or do you prefer a cheque?"

This shut the man up. He just couldn't believe we were buying a brand new car with cash. George also bought an Italian motorbike for himself, and we seemed to be able to materialise whatever we wanted to have. I never understood why he lost it all a couple of years after we broke up. Some things are just never meant to be. He went to Spain and got married there and came back several years later with a daughter and nothing else.

I was still not interested in getting married. I had the idea that when I like a guy, they were not into me, and the ones who were into me were nerds or just not of interest to me for various reasons. The limiting belief "I am not good enough" played out big time in everything in my life, and I did not see it. I was just so eager to please that I must have scared off a lot of people. Another thing I did not realise.

People did like me, but I was so blinded by my belief they did not like me that I couldn't see they actually were very fond of me. I wanted to be popular, and if possible—famous. I imagined cameras following me everywhere, and I could not understand why famous people did not enjoy all that attention. I was craving attention. The more, the better. Even if it made me kiss awful guys, that kind of attention was better than none at all.

I haven't changed a bit. I am still always seeking attention and especially approval. The only thing that has changed is that I am aware of it when I am doing it. Life would be so amazing without any need at all for approval. I would just be myself and approve of myself. No stress to check if others are approving of me as well.

At the age of twelve, I got into a big fight. A boy had been teasing and pestering me in school, and I was so at a loss how to make him see that I was good, not deserving of his spitting on my back and him hurting my hands, hitting them with his schoolbag. I told my father and he said, "You are strong enough to beat the shit out of him. Why don't you go ahead and do that?"

I did as I was told, and a major fight between the two of us broke out. I was holding his head down with my left hand whilst using my right fist to give uppercuts. Blood everywhere. In panic, he lifted his right hand and grabbed onto my hair fiercely, pulling it as hard as he could. I was so out of my mind that I put my teeth in his forearm and bit a piece out of it. Some teachers finally managed to tear us apart, and we had to go and see the principal. I explained that I only did as my father told me to do. Boy, was he ever in trouble! Twenty years later, I ran into this kid now a grown-up man. He said that he was actually very fond of me in those days. He just did not know how to give me attention in a way that I would recognize as the loving kind.

MORE SCHOOL

Life always gives me what I ask for, although the shape in which it presents itself is sometimes a shape I do not recognize as an answer to my prayer. Somehow, I always wanted to reinforce the belief that I am not good enough by doing the things that made me feel bad about myself. Drinking and smoking too much, sleeping around too much, partying too hard—just anything that would really make me feel bad about myself would do to enforce my limiting belief. I dated some guys who really made me feel like a piece of shit and, boy, did I love that! I could not get enough of it. Some borders I did not want to cross. I did not want to do drugs. I was afraid they would damage my brain, and that was something I still valued at a subconscious level. I knew I had a good processor, and it was important to keep that in good shape. I wanted to study sinology, but my father asked if it was something I could eat. He had no idea what it was, so I ended up in law school. I tried very hard to fit in but never did.

I was living together with George by then, and we had a real "couples' life" instead of the wild party life the other university students had. I became so obsessed with fitting in that when I changed university and ended up in Leuven, I only partied there. I couldn't get myself studying again.

During the summer holiday, I had helped out my neighbour who was a lawyer and disliked it enough to know that was something I did not want to be. People fighting and bickering all the time. I might as well go and live with my parents again.

DAILY LIFE—Early Days

George and I grew more and more apart, and, after three months of partying, he wanted out. We had to leave the apartment. For me, that created financial issues, as in no way could I afford to rent on my own. The only solution I saw was to get a job and study at night. For three days and three nights, I moved back in with my parents—or it might have been a week—but as soon as possible, I got my own place and started working.

Most of my earning was commission-based, so I worked my butt off to get it all together. I was very proud to live all by myself at that age and not to have to give explanations to anyone. Towards the end of the month, the money used to get scarce, and I would have to live on bread and sandwich spread. But I was happy. There was no arguing in my house, and the relationship that didn't work was over. I had given myself space for new possibilities.

That is one thing I firmly believe in now: for new things to happen in my life, I need to make space. I will throw away clothes before I buy new ones. Make the space. You want a lover? Don't park in the middle of your two-car spaces; move over and make space. Empty some cupboards so he can put his t-shirts, socks, and undies in there, and make some space for the hangers. It is like in nature—after a bushfire, new life grows much faster. Make room for the things we want in our life.

I will not make room for fear. Fear is something that paralyses and is the opposite of love. In this world, everything needs an opposite, so I guess that is why we have fear, aside from the fact that we have to overcome it. Each time I overcame a fear, I felt stronger and more capable. The need for approval and recognition just faded away. It feels almost better than an orgasm—that feeling of I did this huge scary thing and I made it! Like I made that painting, I got on that very tall horse, I gave up an addiction. Each time the adrenaline flows it feels wonderful.

By feeling the "I can do this, too," I am unleashing my power. I am showing what I can do and what I am. I do not care what other people think. What is important is what I think.

My thoughts are my only concern. And they are also the only thing I can change in this world. I love, especially, to change thoughts that no longer serve me or anyone else for that matter. It usually takes several layers before the core belief is removed or replaced. But when it does—God!—it is the best feeling there is. Suddenly, I am alive again. Even typing about it makes me type faster and makes me feel the pure aliveness of it all. Some might find this all sounds like I am very self-centred, and maybe I am. I made the decision years ago to take the advise we get in airplanes, before take off, how to put the oxygen mask first on our own face before trying to help other people with theirs, literally. In other words I take care of myself first of all.

JOBS

My first job after university was in the food industry. I was a sales rep for a flavour company, and I had no idea what that was. I used to hate sales reps, and, one day, I woke up and I was one. I went to factories trying to sell them vanilla and ham flavor and whatnot. I was representing a brand new department in that company, and they had no idea about the full extent of what they were trying to commercialise. They had hired me to make sure the market would learn about their existence and start buying from them.

I had a briefcase that contained my planner and a price list, and that was it. The price list had no prices, but it was an idea of what kind of things we wanted to market. So I gathered as many samples as I could, had them imitated, and then sold that as an alternative for their present supplier.

My father was selling cacao those days, so we sometimes hit the road together. I did not enjoy it. I got sleepy in the car and always thought I was going to get in trouble or fired. Thought: *I probably should do this better*. In the evenings, I was following marketing courses and on the weekends, I sold furniture in a big shop owned by a friend of my father. I still hated selling. I wanted to be an artist, not someone nicely dressed in a fancy car driving around selling stuff.

After three years, the Belgian market was turning good enough to put in another sales rep, and I became the export manager. Finally, a way to use my languages I learned at school. I travelled frequently to the US, Southeast Asia, and to different countries inside Europe. I still felt empty and dissatisfied. This travelling was not really what I was looking for. I had met another guy, and he didn't like me being away so much, so I contacted a head-hunter who got me in with a major office supplies company. That was worse than anything I could imagine.

I tried to stay on top, but no matter how hard I worked, they made me work harder. They constantly criticised us, thinking that would make us work harder. I got quickly promoted after a couple of months to national account manager and became more and more unhappy. The daily drives in heavy traffic to Brussels; the long, long days and never ending meetings and obligations. We had to keep sheets of how we spent our time during the day by the minute. We had to round hours off, because we were not allowed to work the hours we actually worked.

Their system of doing business too was not straightforward, and it was not congruent with who I was at that moment. My heart was still crying out, *"I want to be an artist."*

I made a deal with the boyfriend that I would quit and start my own business. I wanted an art gallery, not of paintings but other products made by artist. The mother of an ex-boyfriend was working day and night to get in more ideas. She is a real genius in creating objects, clothes, and concepts. I mostly did the executions and did not really like that part. Again, I was missing out too much on the creative part, but I had manoeuvred it that way myself.

The economy started to go really bad, and many galleries in my neighbourhood closed down for a couple of days a week, or sometimes weeks in a row, because no one was buying. I had to sell my penthouse and lost everything I ever worked for. But I did not have to go bankrupt, and I had no debts left whatsoever.

It was a very interesting learning curve, and I learned again how I always opt for the safe way out and could not feed the child/artist within myself who wanted to come out. No, I needed more reassurance and more experience before I would try that one again. Most of all, I needed to change my "thoughts"—my "limiting beliefs"—before my life would get any better.

FAMILY—We All Have One

When I was working hard, I still had the family life running in the background, of course. My mother became more and more depressed after she had an aneurism and suffered from some physical ailments. My father just couldn't stand it anymore. He had met someone else, and he refused to let my mother know. I told him I didn't think it was a good idea to keep it secret, because deep down, people know when these things are happening. He was too happy to finally be loved again that he did not want to take the risk. My mother tried to hang herself with the rope of her bathrobe, but it broke. I visited her in the hospital and felt like a dirty lying cheater for not telling her about the affair my father was having. I was his accomplice in a way, as they sometimes met in my apartment when I travelled overseas, which was the majority of the year. We even went on a business trip together into Germany, and my mother was not allowed to know.

I told my mother to get professional help, and we tried all kinds of things, but she had no interest. She put more and more pressure on me. One day, I snapped. She said, "I will go and do it again, and one of the reasons is that you and your father do not love me." She said that if only I could love her more, she would not be in this situation. I felt like she put an ultimatum on me and did not handle it very well. I told her to make sure this time to use a good rope—we had heaps of them in the garage—and that I would laugh and dance on her grave. That night she hung herself. I did not sing, nor did I laugh, but I was so angry and upset. She blamed everyone but herself. Of course, I felt guilty as hell as well, because she had found out about the affair and me knowing about it. She must have felt betrayed by us. It took me years to get over that anger, and probably ten years before I finally managed to cry. But when I did, I did. It took me another 100 layers of peeling of the onion to get over my guilt. What doesn't kill you makes you stronger. I learned that I was not the cause. I cannot be held responsible for what other people decide to do with their life. They do the best they can do and live in accordance with what they believe to be right or wrong. It is not about me.

LOSSES

By the time I was thirty, I had lost my mother, my apartment, and my dream business, and I was sharing my life with someone who did not want to be committed, and who made me feel like I was somehow not good enough. I took everything seriously and, above all, very personally. I could not see that other people loved me. My past experiences blocked that possibility and prevented me from experiencing love.

I kept thinking it was all about me—and, in a way, it was—but not in the way I thought. I was just trying to do my best and kept fighting and running against the wind instead of going with the flow. I did as I was told by my mother, and made sure my life was a struggle.

We always, always get what we ask for, but we are not always aware of what it is we are asking. Often the conscious and subconscious are directly opposed in what they are asking for, and then we are angry not to get what we were consciously wishing for. We forget the power of the subconscious mind and how it will always win in the end.

Until we become more aware of this and adept in reprogramming our subconscious, we have the impression that life is what happens to us and not the other way around. We are what is happening to life. We are spiritual beings having a bodily experience. I sometimes wish the experience would be more enjoyable, especially when I am in pain. Then again pain is something on the way out; it is no longer inside of us.

It is interesting for sure to have the insights developing as we grow older. How much easier life seems to get when we finally can attract what we want on both levels. When we line up our thoughts and feelings, the power of manifestation is amazing. It just goes on and on. Always giving and never taking back like an Ouroboros, an endless circle biting around and around.

LIFE GOES ON

I tried again to live from my art and started to make paintings of horses and dogs. My partner had to sponsor me a lot, as I had no real income, and I felt worthless. I did a lot of horse riding in those days and also got a truck driver's license to drive him to competitions. I thought I was only good enough to be the driver, and I hardly ever rode competitions. The few times I did, it was not very successful, at least not what I would call a success.

I had a beautiful black stallion to ride dressage with, but I couldn't handle all the pressure. I wanted my independency back, so I started to look for a job again. With a past of the high-profile office supply company, I found one very easily with the competition. I had to start back at the bottom of the ladder, as you do, but I felt satisfied to have my own income again, and no longer be dependent on William. Our relationship got very rocky, and we did not spend much time together. He was very busy with his hobbies. We tried to have the same ones, but it just never worked out. We grew farther and farther apart.

After my mother died, I started to have nightmares in a bad way, and Jim helped me a lot. He could see how my mother was stuck in my aura and how that was pulling me down as well. He taught me the exercise with the light. I sat with a candle in front of me and meditated on someone I loved a lot and projected them in the centre of the flame. Then I projected the adversary in the light as well as myself. I joined all three in the light of the flame and emanated the same loving energy to all three who were joined in the light. It often took several settings, but it has solved many issues in my life.

MORE CHANGE

I was living a life that many envied, and they didn't understand why I wanted a job again. I felt like no matter what I did in the household and the stables, it was never good enough. I felt that I was being lazy, although it took several people to take over what I was doing before, once I started working again. Working for a company outside our house made me feel more in control of my own time. At the same time, it also made me feel safer having my own income again. The spiritual world became more and more real to me, and I knew that it would never be of any importance to my partner. It was what it was, and I took the right decision.

When I went back to work, I also started an aura reading course and energy healing with Ronald van de Peppel. We made a magical trip to Glastonbury, where I became a Reiki master. I was first taken aback with the cost of it, and I had to laugh when they said that the real price to become a Reiki master is so much higher than the money you pay to become one. It was true. Again, I lost the structure to my life as I knew it and was left with some clothes and my easel. I had to leave it all behind to make place for the new.

The old had no place in my new belief system.

I wanted to be free and have a life with a spiritual meaning where I could also help other people. In the situation I was, I did not see that happening. It was stale with no place to go but out. After almost fourteen years, we broke up and I moved out. I had no other place yet, so I moved into my office in town.

Meanwhile, I was working in the maritime industry and running a shipping agency in Antwerp. There was less traffic in the mornings, but still very long days. There was, however, this feeling of being owned by the company. I hardly noticed the difference when I moved into the spare room of the office and my life before I lived there. I was very eager to please my boss whom I also considered as a friend. I felt I needed to be very loyal to her and to whatever crazy thing she would ask me to do. She was a fierce German lady, and she owned the shipping line.

She had worked very hard to get there and was kind of bitter about it all while, at the same time, still feeling like a young girl. She backed me up in my decision to stand on my own feet again, and, at the same time, I was more available than ever. I kept swinging like a pendulum between being spiritually inspired and the business world.

The first months after our break up, I was burning the candle at both sides. It took a very bad fall off a horse to get me back on track. It was like I fell off the merry-go-round, because it was spinning too fast. When I was l lying in the hospital, with probably a broken neck, I thought about where I would go from here. I could move my fingers, and I thought, *No worries; I will just write a book.* At that moment, when I accepted the state I found myself in, I could feel pure, intense blue light flowing through me and encompassing my total being. I was sure it was pure Reiki energy, and I felt my neck being repaired.

The next day, they took another scan, and they said, "No, it is an old crack we saw, not a new one. I did have a nasty fall as toddler from my high chair onto the central heating, and that had left a mark on my bone. I was dismissed out of hospital, but, because I had a severe concussion, I was not allowed to do anything. I had to lie in a dark room for three weeks. Luckily, a friend of mine had just finished renovating their attic into a bedroom, so I could stay there.

I only had my handbag with me, nothing else, at the time of my fall, and all my clothes where in my office. I felt miserable, and every time I tried to move, I needed to vomit. I had time to think about the next step. I was going to get a flat, move out of the office, and start all over again and take it easier. I had turned my life into a merry-go-round, and I just fell off—just in time to avoid something really bad happening. At least that is how it felt.

GETTING IT BACK TOGETHER—Sorting Things Out

The first day I got out of bed after three weeks in the dark, I walked downstairs, and the television was on. It was daytime, and the news was blaring and showing a plane flying into a building. I thought I was still hallucinating or so—but no, it really did happen. That was 9/11. One of those days when you never forget where you were sitting or standing and what you were doing when you heard that so and so died.

That same day, I was back on my feet and went to get a new place to live. It was very close to the place I used to live and to my friends. It was located above horse stables and, from my bedroom, I could hear and see the horses moving around in their box. I loved that

Yes, I Do & I Did It

little attic! It had some quaint furniture in it. The only thing I needed to buy was a bed and some small household stuff. I had my easel up and felt like a king in his castle. I could have books lying around about spiritual subjects without being questioned about my mental health.

Somehow, I still have the belief that atheist people question the mental ability of people who are following a spiritual path. They seem to think we are looking for a drug to ease our mind, and that we are not strong enough without the crutch of a superpower to lean upon. I wonder whether they don't have mystical experiences in which you feel the presence of something bigger than your little self, your ego. Maybe part of me is like an atheist and saying that all this "believing" is just nonsense and mumbo jumbo—all made up by my mind. On the other hand, having a mystical experience is at the core of my being and congruent with what I think I am.

Once I started in that direction of going back to my source, there was no way back. I remember that I made a painting with the writing: "THERE IS NO WORLD" on it. My partner was very upset. I just wanted to be reminded that the world is a dream, because the pain I felt was too big to carry otherwise. So, was I again leaning on a crutch? Or was I finally going to my core feelings and allowing what I really thought life is all about?

Nadine Nelen

AN OLD THOUGHT SYSTEM TO BELIEVE AND TEACH
Basic Assumptions

A body can be destroyed, it is not eternal it is therefore not real. Our Reality is Spirit.

To see the real world we must see the forgiven world. We must see ourselves and everyone as innocent children of God. This is the forgiven world, the real world, and God takes the last step Himself.

The essence of all Creation of God is Love, God is Love.

As Love is the only basis for Reality it can be either asked for or given in great abundance.

Everything we see that is not eternal is illusion. This comes very close to everything we see.

How can we see past this illusion?

By forgiving everyone and everything we see including ourselves. People behaving in illusions know not what they do. They need Love; we need Love because we are One with them.

Results

The results of seeing a forgiven world are peace, light, beauty, unity, charity, kindness, tenderness and all things eternal. The ability to be.

Judgments are impossible within a forgiven world. Anger is impossible within a forgiven world.

A forgiven world has no opposites no degrees of good and bad and nothing prevents it from being what it is, unity in Love. The forgiven world is the eternal sea of life.

The river of life flows to the sea. The forgiven world expands because the source of its expansion - love, is inexhaustible and inevitable. It knows not the illusion of separation.

What is not separated must join. Minds join at the level of the Christ Mind.

They join in enlightment and unconditional love.

Conclusion

God is the Breath of Life

Living does not know death.
Death does not know Life.
Only One is true, death or Life.
Death does not know Love. Love does not know death.
Only One is true. If there is Love then there is no
death. If there is death then here is no Love.

The Breath of Life insures Love.
Know this and all the world is free.
Know this and earth and Heaven are One.

Jim Hill

This is one of the texts Jim would dictate, and I would type out as he spoke. Every Sunday morning, we would meet for breakfast and would work on these articles about a course in miracles. We had long walks with my dog while talking about metaphysics and ACIM. It was a good time, and, at the same time, I was healing a lot of wounds. I felt very, very lonely and unsafe, and I thought, *Just take a spoon of cement and toughen up; you are almost there.*

After living a year and half above the stables and dating some guys who made me feel awful about myself, I started dating someone who was different. Andre made me feel good about myself, for a while at least. We moved in together in a nice house, and the first three months were bliss.

One morning, I woke up with a bad cold, and I asked him to walk my dog. He got very upset, and, for the first time, I saw a stranger. We started to grow apart very quickly, and I realised I had made a big error. In my haste to be in a "perfect" relationship, I had jumped in too fast. We were not suited at all! Our vision of the world was opposed and led to many discussions. Again, it was a good lesson. After that, I waited ten years before I lived in the same house again with my partner. It was a very strange experience that this moving into a house again happened one month after Andre died. May he rest in peace. He was a good man.

After Andre, I met a German man through work, and he lived 400 km away. I was infatuated with him and, of course, blinded again. After dating him for a month of two, I found out he was still married! We were talking on the phone around 11.30 at night. Suddenly, I heard a woman screaming his name—"Helmut!"—and then some stuff I couldn't get, because she was so angry. He hung up on me and only called back two days later. Agony! He had a very sad story, of course, and I always was a sucker for sad stories. He had gone bankrupt, and his wife had started to have an affair with his best friend. They had taken separate bedrooms in the house and lived no longer as man and wife.

I believed him, and after that I kept believing him. Although he seemed to lie a lot to other people, he always had a good reason to do that. I was so blinded again; it was hilarious. He moved out and his wife started to call me and abuse me over the phone. She called my office and told everyone I was a homewrecker. I had to tell her to stop calling me, as she would dial my number 100 times in a row when she was upset. I explained to her that it was considered stalking, and that I would have to take legal action if she continued with that behaviour.

I broke up with Helmut a couple of times, and after the third time or so, it was for good. He had slept with his wife again and lied about that, of course. I had put my heart on moving far away to Australia, and he reacted strangely when I said I was applying for a job overseas. He actually said: "That is great!" In other words, I don't really care that you move even farther away than you already are. We had some great romantic times together, and let's just leave it at that.

After leaving Andre, I lived with a friend for a couple of months. One day, my dog ruined a door in the house, and she decided that the dog was no longer allowed to stay. I had just turned forty and was sitting in the cold in my car with my dog and some clothes. I had no idea where to go. We went for a walk in a beautiful park, and nature, as usual, made me feel peaceful. I thought, *If one door closes, God would open a window.* Within five minutes, I got a phone call from friends asking if I could house-sit for the next two weeks. Our dogs were great friends, and she asked if I could bring my dog along. From there, I went to stay again in the house I lived in with William. He had it up for sale and did not want it empty. He had moved in with a new partner. They split up after six months, and he moved back in the house where I was living meanwhile. It was kind of strange to share a house with a former partner, but we got along just fine and still do. We laughed when we realised how funny it would have looked to the neighbours—me moving out then he moving out, and me back in and then he back in. A typical romantic comedy playing out in real life.

I worked many years for the same shipping company, and the last year was very difficult. I also had enough of Belgium, and I wanted to go and live in a warmer climate and change absolutely everything in life. The relationship with Helmut was turning pear-shaped, and I decided to go and follow my own dreams alone and look for a job overseas, as far away as possible from all this madness and to finally live a life that I always desired. I drew up the exact things that I wanted, and I just knew I was going to make it happen.

THE WISH LIST

Life was getting more and more stressful: heavy traffic everywhere; rain, rain, and more rain; shitty people; worries about work, money, relationships, and family. I would say the usual. I heard a lot of people complain, and I did the same, but I realised I wanted change. Relationships were not working out the way I wanted. My work was making me sick with stress, and the winters were too cold and too long. I took a piece of paper and wrote down ten things I was grateful for in the last year and ten things I wanted to do in the next year. I even made some drawings around the words while envisioning how it would feel to have those things come true. I would, every so often, take out that piece of paper and look at them and align my feelings with living that life that I had written on paper. On the second of November 2005, I wrote down the following list:

1. Peace of mind
2. World peace
3. Happiness
4. A life that truly inspires me; a life of passion that I approach with gusto
5. LOVE (no fear)
6. A job I adore
7. A house to call "my home"; my own place where I can safely be myself
8. Good health (and lose ten kilos)
9. Enough time to go to the beach, shop, read, sing, dance and have fun
10. The money to pay for all of this

When I now look at that wish list I am amazed how, in one way or another, I have manifested the essence of my list. Since I wrote that one, I have become more elaborate on how I make them, and the results are stunning. Thanks to the workshops and treasure mapping from my dearest friend, Deborah Sammon, I now have a much clearer idea about how to make a vision board/wish list.

Anyway, one day, I was reading the Antwerp Lloyd shipping newspaper and saw an advertisement for a job in Brisbane, Australia. I had been in Australia ten years earlier and had visited Sydney and Port Douglas, but I had never even heard of Brisbane. So I looked it up and thought, *Wow! That is exactly what I am doing. I am going to move heaven and earth to get that job. That job is mine, and I am going to live in Australia.* I applied and arranged for the first interview, which was held in Hamburg. I was so excited to fly there and made sure I gave a calm and collected impression to show the professional side of me. It went great and a second interview was set for a month later.

AUSSIE, AUSSIE, AUSSIE, OI OI OI

In total, it took almost a year before I got the final interview, which was in Brisbane. It was nerve-wracking, all that waiting and not knowing whether I would be moving to the other side of the world or not, but it was worth every second of it. I was suffering from chronic back pain. The flight was painful, but the painkillers they gave me were so strong that they made me hallucinate. So I didn't want to take them again, or else they might make me jump out of the plane or make a complete fool of myself.

On the second leg, I was sitting next to a man, and we started chatting. I was so positive that everything I saw was through rose-coloured glasses. I thought we really clicked, that it was amazing that things were happening so fast, and that even before I landed, I would already have met the Australian I knew I would one day meet. Little did I know then that this guy, Stephen, was a "Pommy." (Australians refer to "English" people as Pommy. In the early days, when the convicts arrived in Australia from England, they had a shirt that said "POM"—Prisoner of her Majesty. Some say it is because English people have very pale skin, and it turns red like a pomegranate in the sun.) We exchanged numbers, and I promised I would let him know when I would be at the Gold Coast to catch up for coffee. I was planning to take a bit of break while in Australia, so after the job interview, I would drive to the Gold Coast and then to the Sunshine Coast to have some beach holidays.

The interview went very well, and the people all seemed so friendly compared to the Germans I used to work with. So I thought, *Finally, Nadine, you are starting to get your shit together.* The job was not the one I originally applied for, but it was the same money, so I didn't care. The guy who hired me said; "it is a shame you are not a man because you are better suited for the job then the French bloke I hired for this job but this is the shipping industry and I can't risk having a woman in that position". To me the only thing that mattered at that moment was that I was in Australia, and that I was going to spend the rest of my life here. The papers were signed, and they would apply for a working permit.

Meanwhile, I had to go back to Belgium to get some more clothes. It was Christmas and it was bloody hot. I went to Dicky Beach on Christmas Day at six o'clock and was enjoying the heat of the sun already. The lifesavers were wearing red Santa hats and long white beards. The poor buggers, they must have been sweating like hell. I thought; *If this is winter here in Australia, imagine how good summer will be!* I did not realise that the seasons are the opposite on the opposite side of the world, and that it was actually full on summer. So when I packed my suitcases to come back to work, I only took summer gear and left all the winter clothes with my sister. When I went a to Melbourne in June that year, I regretted it a bit and had to buy a nice warm jumper. They even ski in Australia in winter. I never thought that would be possible, but there are snowy mountains here.

The work permit was not yet ready, but I had my flight back already booked which caused me to come in as a tourist at the border that gave me three hours of delay, as they wanted to make sure I would not start to work until I had the permit. It took three months before I got it. Meanwhile, I couldn't get paid. Luckily, I had some savings to carry me through those months. I was renting a fully furnished unit, which are very common in Australia. It was strange to live with the sword of Damocles hanging above my head like that. Being on a work permit meant that if I lost my job, I had only twenty days to leave the country. It often stressed me out, but I decided that I would wait the necessary two years it takes to get my permanent residence. I was very determined to stay in the country of my dreams whatever it would take!

WORKING IN AUSTRALIA

When I arrived in the office; they pointed me to a desk and gave me a laptop, a mobile phone, and keys to a beautiful brand new car. "This is it," they said. "Here you go." The working area was open plan, and I was used to having my own big spacious office. So, suddenly, it was strange, with all these people sitting around me, making phone calls, and talking loudly. I was so happy to be in Australia that nothing—absolutely nothing else—mattered. The fact that they treated me like I was a spy sent from the German head office, that I had no friends or family here; it was all in the perspective of following my dream. When the political backstabbing in the office was really bad, I would go into the restrooms, cry a bit, and get back to work. Same in the evenings. I would sometimes be so upset with events in the office that I cried myself to sleep.

The man from the plane, Stephen and I had arranged to catch up again and we had dinner. I really liked him, and we talked a lot on the phone. But somehow, the second dinner took ages to happen. He was mostly talk, but I couldn't see, and I just thought he was very busy like me. I lived in the city centre for the first six months with amazing views over the Brisbane River and the Story Bridge.

I spend the first weekends alone in the botanical gardens across the street or went to the coast for a drive or just wandered through the city. My back was still very painful, but I had found a wonderful chiropractor. In one year, he had it completely fixed. Through customer functions organised by the company I worked for I met people, and one of them became a good friend. She was a very loud and ocker Aussie, but I enjoyed her company. She knew how to have a party and have good fun.

When my six-month lease for my first apartment was coming up, she asked if we could maybe share accommodation. The rents are very high, and she had just lost her house. I had never done that, so I thought, *Why not? I would give it a try.* We rented a big loft on the river in Teneriffe. It was strange to live with someone, and her son was very weird. He would stand in my bedroom in the middle of the night, very creepy. I love my quiet moments, and always having the radio blaring, the television on, and her talking on the phone with a loud voice would irritate me. Then, when I found the drugs her son had brought in the house in my cooler handbag, I freaked out and said: "No I am leaving to go and live by myself again." I found another place and rejoiced living alone again.

I had seen a bit more of Stephen, but he was difficult to grasp. I had tickets for the finals of a rugby game in Sydney and since he used to live there, I thought I might invite him along. We went for the whole weekend. That Saturday, we went shopping, and he saw a dress he wanted me to try on. It was a very nice cream-coloured silk dress from a French designer. He said: "this is so you; you have to wear this dress," and took out his wallet and walked to the counter. I understood he wanted to do something back, as the tickets were over seven hundred dollars each, but when I looked at the price tag on the dress and I was surprised to see it was almost three thousands dollars.

He had always given the impression he was a very successful businessman, so for him that might not have been an issue. The lady in the shop wrapped up the dress while I changed back into my clothes, and when I arrived at the counter Stephen had walked out and was talking into his mobile phone—still holding his wallet. The lady was very friendly, and we had been chatting in French. She said, "Here is the dress all nicely wrapped up, but he hasn't paid yet."

We chatted a bit longer, but then a painful silence arrived. I did not want to lose face so I thought, *What the heck,* and pulled out my wallet and gave her my credit card.

She said, "How strange. I also had the impression he was going to pay, but then he just walked out."

I was fuming and very angry when I walked out that shop. I became very silent.

He offered to buy me lunch in that same shopping centre. We sat down and I ordered a pasta dish. I needed comfort food—and urgently! I did not want to show my emotions, so I pretended all was good.

The next date we had, he stood me up, so I broke up with him. A couple of weeks after that, I went to Melbourne for the horse races, the famous "Melbourne Cup." I thought, *Great, I can wear that ridiculously expensive dress for that.*

While I was there, he called me. He was a smooth talker, so we made up over the phone. He said, "When you get back, I will take you out to a surprise dinner. And could you please wear that dress so I can see you in it?" I did and when he picked me up, I was dressed up to the nines and beaming proudly. We arrived in the city in the neighbourhood of all the nice restaurants, and he parked his car. I thought how wonderful that he chose a place in this area. I like most of the restaurants around here, and I was curious to see which one he had chosen. He said, "Let's first have some drinks in the Stamford hotel."

So in we went. Surprise! All the people from his company were sitting there. I immediately noticed how overdressed I was compared to them, as most of them were in jeans and t-shirt, not even a shirt.

Great start Nadine, well done!

After the drinks, we all—yes, all fifteen of us—went next door to the Japanese restaurant. It is one of these bar grills where the cook stands in the middle cooking on a hot plate and the customers sit around him. Part of the attraction is that the cook sometimes throws the food in the air so that the customers can catch it in their bowls. Our cook was very good at it, but I am a bad catcher. So when he threw the rice and egg at me to catch in my bowl, it went all over my dress. They thought it was hilarious, so I got thrown some more food my way, and most landed on the dress.

"No worries," Stephen said, "I will pay for the dry cleaners."

"Like you were going to pay for the dress to begin with?" I said.

He had this weird explanation that he did not pay for the dress because he wanted to let me be in my own power. He said, "You must be making some good money and worth quite a bit, so I did not want to offend you by buying a dress for you."

I still find it hard to believe. I kept seeing him, but I wonder where my right mind was hiding at that time…

He did some more weird, unexplainable stuff, and I wrote him an e-mail with all the questions I had and reasons that I no longer wanted to see him. I said that the whole situation was a catch-22 and that I opted out. After three months, he came back with a reply, typed in red behind my questions. He also wondered if I would be interested in catching up with him. I answered back in one short message. "Sorry, catch-22 has turned into a Harvey Norman situation."

He said, "What does that mean?"

I came back with, "Absolutely no interest for the next 24 months." (Harvey Norman is a big retail store chain in Australia that charges no interest for two years on purchases made, and, in those days, they were blaring out this catchphrase on the radio and television every five minutes.)

I wore that dress only one more time at a birthday party I had given for myself. A girlfriend, as a joke, sat on my lap and stuck her tongue in my mouth. I convulsed and the glass of red wine I was holding in my hand got spilled all over the cream-coloured silk, ruining the dress forever. Only recently did I finally threw it out, as I kept hoping to get the stain out or the have it dyed in another colour, but it was only meant to be used three times.

MOVING TO THE SEASIDE

I moved outside Brisbane to be closer to the water and started to commute every day to work. I loved my morning walks along the beach. We had a group of three women who would walk on the concrete footpath that runs along the shore to Redcliffe and back, and often the sun was already scorching at seven in the morning, so we would leave at five thirty. I made sure to be ready by seven thirty to go and commute into the city.

I didn't mind driving into the city every day. Being in my car for over an hour on my way to work allowed me to listen to my tapes of Eckard Tolle, Byron Katie, and Kenneth Wapnick. They really inspired me. My health was not so good, and I started to get problems with asthma and allergies. I saw a naturopath and she said, "This job is slowly killing you. Due to stress you are no longer digesting properly, and all is out of wack." I was put on severe diets to clean out my system, and I lost a lot of weight that time.

I did not have weekly discussions with Jim, but I did try to stay connected with ACIM. I had started an account on Facebook and reconnected with some people I went to school with in Europe.

The world seems smaller and smaller these days, and, no matter where we are, we can stay in contact. I found what I did very normal, because I lived it every day, but former friends could see it was something special to follow your dreams and just move on. Most people, even when in a rut, prefer to stick to the devil they know. I always opted for change, perhaps to quickly. Then again that was okay, I always had all the chances I needed to adapt, learn and move on.

I started to heal myself little by little and created some more wounds with my modus operandi in the dating world. I thought I was seeing this guy who was much younger than I, and not normally someone I would fall for. One morning, I was lying at the pool in our building, and he had the sliding door open from his apartment. Next thing I saw was a woman stepping out of his bed. I was devastated and felt humiliated at the same time. To top it off, they came to the pool and sat around as well. I hid behind a pair of huge sunglasses and a hat. Later on, I confronted the guy. He said he understood it was clear for me that between us, it was just good fun and nothing else. I was not good at "just fun," as I get involved emotionally when I sleep with someone. So I had to stop seeing him.

Then I ran into a Belgian bloke when I was in New Orleans for work, and we had a fling that ran very hot. He had huge mood swings. I found out later he was on drugs, both legal and illegal, and that felt very disturbing. After I travelled to Belgium in the

Yes, I Do & I Did It

wintertime just to see him, and he didn't show up, I realised I was still dating losers. I didn't realise I was not ready to start dating boyfriend material, so I was dating the ones who are just playing the field and that are damaged goods just as I was. I thought I was over my past relationship hurts, and I couldn't see I was still stuck in old pain and limiting beliefs. The wounds were deep, and I cried a lot. I felt not worthy of love and was sure I would never ever find someone who would love the real me and not the image I projected of me. On the outside, I was the hard and self-reliant businesswoman; but on the inside, I was this little insecure girl reaching out in all the wrong places to be held and to be loved. Ridiculous, but that was how it was. Now I can see that I was the cause why these guys just used me to have some fun. I was eager to please, available and let it all happen.

After two years on a working permit, I hired a specialised immigration lawyer to help me with the application for permanent residence. We made it. It was not easy. I had to do the English IELTS test and various medical checkups, like giving urine samples with a witness present…all good fun! Or as the Aussie saying goes, "She'll be right, mate."

I started to look around for another job, and a man who used to work as a consultant for us wanted to hire me. He was an agent for a company that had a great fleet, and it was all project work. We talked for a while, and I felt it was the right thing to do. I should switch to his company.

He was off to the other side of Australia to run his office from over there, and his PA and I would work from Brisbane. He said, "You don't need a contract, you know? When I give my word it is good; no need to put it in writing."

I said, "You might be right, but I really need a contract for me, so I would feel better about myself."

I wrote up the contract myself, and we both signed it. I went to work for him. Leaving the offices of the other company felt wonderful. I was so unhappy there that I could not imagine working there for another day.

When I came to Australia, I had the idea that all would be different here. I thought that if I travelled such a distance to start my life again, for sure, it could not be anywhere near the life I was leading before. The opposite side of the world will give me the opposite experience, and guess what? Nothing changed at all. What I had forgotten was that I had taken my mind with me, and that all the problems I have in this world come from that mind and not from the outside. What a beautiful lesson that was: only I am responsible for what happens to me, and no one or nothing else is.

There is never anyone we can blame for anything we experience as bad, sad, or hurting. We are 100 percent the cause of our kind of existence, our experiences, and our feelings. In my old thinking way, I used to say: "I am feeling sad, because you did this and that to me." Now I think, *I am feeling sad, okay. Why am I not giving myself the space to be happy in?* If I don't like the behaviour of people around me, I will get out of that situation, but I have no reason to blame them

Yes, I Do & I Did It

for anything. Usually, I am very aware that whatever other people make me feel is a lesson for me, not a curse. I am the one asking to be taught this lesson, and the other agreed to play that role.

Maybe we made contracts before coming in this life with other souls to teach each other lessons and to help each other to reach our destination. Some very courageous souls take on the role of the bad guys, so we can learn how not to be. A blind drunk teaches us more than a pious, sober man about alcohol use and abuse. These souls take the other side of the coin. I wouldn't like to put my hand up to play that role. These days, I prefer to play the "good guy." During regressions, I had memories of lifetimes where I did awful things and the subsequent "karma" that I made myself go through afterwards. I relived all this to make me see that whatever I do to another I do unto myself. At the level of oneness, there is no other and all is one.

When I started in the new job, I felt like I had finally landed in heaven. I had finally made it and was exactly where I wanted to be. I worked my ass off to make sure I could fix cargo, and, after four months, I booked the first project ship. I was over the moon as I had gotten up in the middle of the night a couple of times to call with the head office in Europe and to make sure I did the right thing for the customer.

I had also started dating a new guy, and he seemed perfect. My life could not get any better! Then one morning, I arrived in the office, and the PA gave me a letter. I started reading it, and, basically, it said: "Pack your personal stuff, give your car keys and phone to my

PA, and leave the office for good. Here is a check with a month wages." I felt like I was hit by truck. This was not happening! I loved my job! I had just closed a great deal, and I got fired? Me? The phone number from my mobile phone used to be my private one, and all my contact details were in my phone, so I was shocked that I had to give it to them. I also had just bought an apartment and was stuck with a big mortgage.

I called my boyfriend to pick me up. I was like in shock when he drove me home, and he seemed a bit standoffish. I thought, I'll worry about that later. It was close to my birthday, and I had invited lots of people. I actually wanted to cancel it all. I contacted a top lawyer, and, thanks to my contract, I got what I was owed and my phone back in my name. I could start thinking about what next.

The boyfriend was actually not anywhere near what I saw in him. I am specialised in seeing all these wonderful things in people that I wish were there, and the reality is that they are completely different. I just make them up to be my ideal partner and do not test that with what is real. He was no longer happy with me having a high paying job, so the day before my birthday, we broke up. From driving a nice Audi A6, I went to buy a Toyota Corolla of seventeen years.

The good thing was I had heaps of time to spend on self-reflections, sports, walking along the water, meditation and commuting with nature. Nature is always such a great consoler for me. A good beach and big waves can heal any pain or sorrow, and it gives fewer headaches than a bottle of wine. During these walks on a beach I can feel the power that exists in the universe. The mighty waves that crash down—they are soft as they consist of water, but, at the same time, they can eat away mountains or knock you to the ground if you don't keep an eye on them.

The energy I feel when I am connected is the same one as when I went to this ashram of Babaji in Omaha. In those days, I had a guru that I felt very connected to, and the level of devotion would bring me to tears. Even today, when I listen to the Haarati, the tears come back from the depth of my being; my whole soul weeps. It taught me that this is all me! I am not just this little me that I see in the mirror; I am so much more then that. I am one with everything that surrounds me.

I am looking forward to being able to get that same feeling of oneness and peace with all the people who are in a shopping centre trying to get a parking place around Christmas time.

MY OWN BOSS AGAIN

Because shipping jobs are not easy to get in the area I lived, I decided to start my own company. I had a friend who was very knowledgeable in the saddle industry, and she said, "People often ask if we have horsy handbags. Why don't you make them? You are very creative, and they can make them in China for you."

I decided to go to Guangzhou and make a whole collection of handbags for horse lovers. I love China—the smells, the food, the hustle and bustle, the different culture, and the amazing language that I want to learn one day. The whole thing, it attracts me. It is dichotomy at a top level.

The hotels are so cheap compared to Australia, and they offer great quality. I started to produce the handbags with a Spanish bloke, Enrico, who ran a handbag production factory there. I showed him my designs, and we went together to the markets to choose the materials. He was going to make some samples and send them to me. Meanwhile, I had to send him some money. I did send the money and waited, waited, and waited…

I got sick and tired of waiting, which even on a good day is not my best attribute, and flew back to China.

As soon as I arrived, I had the feeling something was not kosher. Enrico had people chasing him for money everywhere. I was in his office, and he had to go into the meeting room with a whole bunch of Chinese people. I heard noises coming out of the room that did not sound like they were having a civilised meeting. Enrico came out all ruffled, with bruises on his neck, and without his passport. They had confiscated the passport until he paid. If he did not pay, they would come back to cut off a finger. Great! And this guy owed me money, too. I thought I would just stick around and make sure that the money he was expecting to come in was used to buy the material for my handbags. I also needed another company to make the handbags; it was clear that his business would be closed down any moment. Enrico was a great guy to hang out with. Every day we went to the markets and looked at all the materials. My creative mind was loving every minute of it.

Those markets are amazing. There are whole buildings several stories high, and each one specialising in something different. One only sells materials to make shoes, the one next door only sells buttons, then another one specialises in real leather, and so on and so on. One day, Enrico got money in from another customer, so I made sure to go with him. He took it out of his account in US, and then we had to go to markets were they sell fake watches to have it changed into Renminbi (Chinese currency). They have money-counting machines under the counter and probably make ten times more in money-changing than selling watches. The stacks of renminbi that I saw were enormous.

We had found a manufacturer, and he started to make more samples for me to approve. A visit that was originally for only ten days lasted for over a month, but I saw the first handbags coming out of the production roll.

Together with my friend from the saddle industry, we drove around Australia visiting all kinds of places. We ran from store to store, both in the major cities and in country towns. Australia is so beautiful and full of variety and best seen from a car I find. I would have loved those road trips if it weren't for the fact we were always running and in a hurry. One day, I would like to do this at a more leisurely pace and really take it all in. My friend from the leather industry—who organised all these trips—came along, and we had heaps of fun. The handbags were selling like cupcakes, so I went back to

China to order more. I had doubled and tripled the order based on previous sales. I was confident, although it stretched me out financially—I was on a winner. I had a job where I could be creative. I made lots of drawings of horses that were placed on the outside of the handbags and also designed the models of the handbags. The job also allowed me to travel and regularly spend time in China.

Back in Australia, we went on the road again, and guess what? The GFC (general financial crisis) hit, and my sales dropped heavily. I seem to have a knack of starting a new business just before some major general financial crisis takes place. Good timing!

I had to look for another income, as I was stuck with a serious mortgage. And at the rate my sales were going, I was running dry fast.

I spoke with my friend whom I have since I arrived in Australia, and she said, "Why don't you see online what is available in disability service? You would be very good working with people with a disability. It is a twelve-hour shift on a casual basis. It also has night shifts, so it leaves you time to keep running the handbag business."

I thought that was a wonderful idea and applied with the disability services for a job as residential caretaker. I got in and immediately started the training.

It was very interesting what we were taught, but the only thing was that, during the breaks, I had to do the phone calls and invoices for the handbags. I was so busy that I had no time for a private life. It was always in the back of my head that one day, I would start dating again and find someone to share my life with. But that would have to wait.

The job of residential caretaker brought out the best and worst in me. I couldn't believe the smell in some of the houses, as they were not always cleaned to high standards, and most of the people we had to take care of were incontinent. It takes a while before your stomach gets used to changing diapers for a grown-up on medication. I repeated "what does not kill me makes me stronger" a zillion times, and put some more lavender oil on my upper lip. I learned to do things without breathing through my nose.

The worst part is that you are not allowed to talk about how you sometimes get shocked during the day from what happens. It made me feel like an outcast, and I could sympathize with how Vietnam veterans feel when they would say that society didn't really want to know their stories as they are too horrible. I remember a friend of mine getting angry and saying to me, "I am too sensitive. You can't talk about your job; it is disgusting." However, I needed to vent to digest it myself. Sharing the horror stories of that job made me feel human again. I was lucky to have one friend who would listen and console me. It helped me put it all in perspective.

I worked with nonverbal autistic people mostly, and the furniture in the house was all bolted down in case they had an anger attack. We used to call it "a behaviour", and we had to record them all. There were hours of paperwork to record absolutely everything. It became such a habit that more than once, after I came home from a twelve-hour shift and after going to the toilet, I would start looking for the sheet to note the time and consistency of the bowel movement. On one shift, I was cleaning tons of poo again from the bathroom floor, trying not to breathe through my nose and not to listen to the screaming and banging. I thought, *Is this why I studied so much and learned to speak five languages? Is this what it all boils down to?* Very humbling.

At the same time, I had great moments there when I could manage to get the best out of a customer after building a rapport. I noticed very quickly that although our customers couldn't talk, they were very intelligent and knew exactly how to play you. They were perfect mirrors of my internal state. I used to meditate before going inside the house to make sure I didn't bring in any confusion, anger, or upset in my energy. It was as if they could read your aura, and they would use it to their advantage or to give you a very hard time until you broke down. We were bounded by very strict rules, and the management was not very nice. They were all specialised in micromanagement and not always open to change.

I tried to get a lot of night shifts even though we had to stay awake all night in case there were any "behaviours," but they allowed time to travel around with the handbags. The business was selling less and less handbags, and I had few returning customers. I missed my days in shipping, so when a good mate of mine retired and asked me if I was interested in his job, I said I would love to take it over. He worked for a small shipping company based in Sydney, and, as the Queensland manager, could work from home and travel often to the Pacific islands.

The salary was not what I used to earn before, but what the heck. It was better than cleaning poop all day, and it would give me that safe feeling again of having a steady job.

There were lots of candidates for the job, and I was in heaven when I made it. I started full of enthusiasm and was delighted to finally be back in shipping and on the wharf, ships, and planes. I thought, *Bring it on! It is all so beautiful. I have a great boss—the best one I ever had, and no commuting to work. How good can life get?* While I was on a roll, I would make time to date again as well!

DATING IN AUSTRALIA

My dating stories are ample to fill a whole book by itself. Even though they say, "once bitten, twice shy," I continued. I thought I will persevere, true to my stubborn nature, and I will find a suitable partner this time.

Let me start with some of the things that had happened before, in the early days of my new Australian life. The first time I tried Internet dating was after I had been living in Australia for three years. I had found a Web site that most people used. My friends took beautiful pictures of me, and I wrote my profile. It was Boxing Day, and I was on leave, so I went online. Very soon, a guy called Adam started chatting with me.

What a coincidence! I thought. *The first man who is contacting me is the first man who ever got a name. Would I be like Eve?*

I could see his picture and read some text, but there was not much there. We had a chat online, and his typing was either slow or he was attending to several chats at the same time. He was wearing sunglasses on the profile picture, and someone had told me to never trust that fact. He asked me out for coffee that day at four, and I had nothing else on, so I said, "Yes, sure. See you at four at the public place, the coffee club." He e-mailed me an hour later, saying he forgot to tell me that he had an aneurism a couple of years ago and that he still spoke with an accent due to that. I replied, "No worries, I have an accent, too, a European one."

I told my friends where I was going and with whom, put on a dress and high heels, and left. Upon arrival, I saw a disabled man leaning against the wall, and he had problems keeping his balance. When I got closer, he seemed to say my name, so I turned around and said, "Pardon?"

"Na-na-ana-aa-ddd-ine," he repeated with a very difficult-to-understand stutter. He was swaying like a drunk while flapping with one hand in all directions.

"Yes," I said. "Can I help you?"

"A-a-a-a-a-a-dam," he said.

I suddenly understood that he was my date. In a daze, I followed him to a table, and, on the way, he stumbled over some chairs and almost tipped another table over. If this was just an accent, then what else was he being dishonest about? We sat down, and I noticed he hadn't even bothered to dress up nicely. He was wearing awful sandals; his toes with purple fungus-eaten nails sticking out. The waitress came and she, too, could not understand him. He tried to order a cappuccino, and I understood what he tried to say before the waitress did. She kept scratching her hair and looking at me to translate. When he got the coffee, most of the froth ended up on his chin and cheekbone as he was waiving it dangerously all over the place. He could not control his movements at all.

I stayed one hour as promised but could not understand him very well, and the energy he emanated was very scattered. He asked for my phone number and I said, "I don't think that is a good idea. I can't understand you even when lip-reading, let alone over the phone. My English is not up to this." I could not believe he had not been more open and honest about his "accent" and called a spade a spade. Anyway, it was a clear warning and an example that everyone on the Internet is not always who they pretend to be. On the other hand, I was not being honest with him. I did not tell him that he should be more real about his situation. I thought it would be better to be the nice girl and not say anything that might be harmful. Now I think I should have been honest and not sat there for an hour, knowing all the time I was going to leave. He might have been lead on by my "nice", but dishonest, behaviour.

It was the beginning of trial and error, waiting in vain for people to get back to me. Some guys were getting upset I didn't answer their e-mails with the speed they expected. It was like a jungle with unknown rules and hidden pitfalls. To assist me with getting a grasp on the subject of finding a suitable partner, I did what I always do. I bought heaps of books about the subject and read them all. Some were helpful, some were less. My favourite one that gave me the best results was *Cosmic Love* from Yasmin Boland. She is an Australian astrologer, and I also love reading her posts on the Internet. The book had lots of exercises that one can do to attract love in your life. I followed them up, especially the ones about making space and decluttering your life. I cleaned my flat from top to bottom, moved stale energy out of every corner, and wrote pages and pages to make sure my mind was a in good shape to attract the right type of person for me. I became aware of the many unresolved issues I needed to sort out before I would be able to find the right man and have things change in my life.

I probably went through her book three or four times, and, each time, I got rid of another layer. Whenever friends of mine are looking for good advice about how to get into the right shape when looking for a partner, I point them towards this book.

There were many trials and errors of dating. After the Adam episode, there was "the lolly man." We spoke over the phone, and I knew he liked to be healthy, and that he walked his dog every day. He seemed very nice and friendly. We agreed to meet at the movies, and, when I first saw him, I realised I had made a mistake. The energy field did not feel compatible to me. He was shorter than me, but that did not bother me as much. He had a plastic holder with him, and I wondered if he had brought his own food to the theatre. He saw me looking at it and said: "I brought these lollies for you. I got them for Christmas, and I don't eat lollies, so I thought you might like them." I couldn't believe my ears. Had he only eaten his favourite colour out of them? They obviously were no longer in the original bag. I declined, as I do not like sweets, and wondered if I should buy some nice hot popcorn or chips instead.

Upon arrival at the ticket counter, he said, "I have a voucher for a reduction, so you only need to pay five dollars."

I thought, *What a cheap skate*, and pulled a fiver out of my wallet. The movie was great, but sad at the same time. We watched *Marley and Me*, and movies with dogs always make me cry. I was very conscious of him sitting there and of his dead-rabbit smelling breath, so I did not get too involved in the sad parts. I just promised myself to cry later. After the movie, he wanted to meet me again, but I just said, "I don't think so," and I ran to my car and bawled my eyes out for the next ten minutes.

After the lolly man, there was the "closet man," Greg. We met the first time during speed dating. The worst experience I ever had! I thought it was a wine-tasting evening I had signed up for, together with a friend. Later, it seemed I had paid to go and partake in a speed-dating event. There had been some kind of a mix up, and the wine-tasting tour was on another day. They put the women in a category with all men ten to twenty years their senior, and there were way more women than men to begin with. I had not lied about my age, as they suspect most people do, and that put me at the table with the geriatrics. Whenever you see a movie with a funny scene about speed dating, know that it is exactly the way it is. Nothing is exaggerated in those dating movies.

Somehow, I managed to get to another table with people my age and had a nice chat with Greg. I didn't leave my phone number, as I was not in the mood. The experience had left me depleted, and I made sure that next time there would be wine tasting involved. That way, I could forget about my troubles. On a Sunday, a couple of weeks later, I went on one of those tours and run again into Greg again. He remembered me, and we got along like a house on fire.

He was a country boy and had some cows. I liked his slow walk and typical farmer behaviour, just like in the series *The Farmer Wants a Wife*. He only owned boots to wear on his feet, so I had to go and buy him shoes to take him to a function related to my work. He kept referring to them as "poofter" shoes. I got to meet some of his family. His former sister-in-law had a kid who looked a lot like him, and, at first, he denied any rumour. I found out the DNA tests were ordered, and he also had other kids somewhere else. Suddenly, I ended up in the middle of an Australian soap, with lies and deceit everywhere.

Although we had spent some time together, we had only "consummated" the relationship once. He mostly just wanted to cuddle. It was strange, as I never had met a man who was like that. He had a big chip on his shoulder about gay men and made many remarks about them. Then, a week after we broke up, while I was cleaning out my wardrobe closet, I got a text from him—a very short one. It said: "I am gay." After forty years, he finally came out of the closet! He must have faced his final lie and decided to move on with it.

During those ten years of dating, the longest lasted six months. He was a very nice lawyer and lived 80 km away from me. He had read some books about spirituality and was into healthy living. We also went salsa dancing together. He used to dance a lot and knew all the moves, but I never had the guts to tell him I thought he was not a good dancer. He was very stiff, and his hands were hard and bony as a rock. I prefer to dance with someone who has firm hands with butter inside. They probably would be great dressage horse riders, too, as the reins are held in a very similar way—firm but gentle. Not hard as bone, pushing you around without any feeling. He was very nice, so I didn't want to hurt his feelings and never mentioned this.

He had a very well developed feminine side, which suited me fine in the beginning, and then it started to annoy me. It was in a way very similar to my experience with Greg, and I could not see him as man I wanted to grow old with. I suspected again that he might not really be into women and had the final talk with him. He went dark with anger and must have felt extremely offended. I just tried to give my honest feelings. We even went to counselling together. The counsellor said that it was my entire fault, and that I was the one being too masculine. *Nihil novi sub sole*, I thought. As long as he could be happy, that was all that mattered to me.

Next thing I know, he moved into a place next to where I had just bought an apartment, and the stalking started.

It was very uncomfortable, although he never crossed any legal lines. He always had a legitimate reason to be in my neighbourhood, so there was nothing I could do. He just followed me around and looked out of his window to check if I was at the pool or on the beach. I ran into him when I did my grocery shopping and other things like that. He lived there for two years and had to drive the distance every day to work. Last time I saw him, he was with a beautiful blond girl, and I do hope they are very happy now.

It is so frustrating to meet so many people you are not compatible with. The few who made it to the next step, where it passed into something physical, were even worse. As soon as they had sex, the game playing started. Lots of excuses genre: "I dropped my six thousand dollar flat screen television, and I am too angry to see you"; "My father is dying of cancer" (the man in question is still alive years later); "My uncle has an incurable disease"; "I lost my phone"; "My battery was flat"; anything really.

None of them had the balls to say: "Listen, I am just not that into to you." That was what it all came down to; they were not that into me, and I did not see that or they did not want to hurt my feelings. They did me a great favour, and l learned a lot from these guys. I made a new plan of attack. I read the book *He's Just Not That*

Into You a couple of times and got the message. I had to make myself less available and be choosier. Learn to love myself first; the rest would follow.

LESSONS IN LOVE

I read somewhere that the love of my life is the one who is looking into my eyes every morning when I look into the mirror. Love is not external. Love is everywhere; it is my essence. I just need to connect with it to experience it. My true being is made out of life force, and it is an endless source that can keep pouring out love without ever running dry. There cannot be any scarcity of love. The only thing that happens is that sometimes I cut myself off from the awareness of love. Sometimes I choose not to see the light and to stay in the darkness. Sometimes I just want to wallow in self-pity and feel really bad about myself. Sometimes I get very insecure and act foolishly. Then I have regrets and the need to punish myself for my stupid mistakes. Because the universe is so friendly, that is exactly what I will be getting.

The key is to know when and how to turn this around. The mind can be trained to pick up on this self-destructing behaviour, as well as to install new and healthier habits than beating oneself up. The sooner you pick them up, the faster they run and the less they have the need to reappear in your life. In the end, we are in control of our lives. We are the director and the actor at the same time, and we can change the movie anytime we see fit. Not by fiddling with the screen where the movie is projected upon but to go to the place where the projector stands and inspect the projector, a.k.a. our mind. Any mistakes happening on the screen originate from the projection. That is where the cause to the action we perceive on the screen lies. The cause is only relevant here in duality. Once we turn back to our original state, there is no cause. Everything just is, so there is also no effect. On this level of our existence, we still think in cause-and-effect mode, and then that is what we perceive all around us. Without that belief, we probably would not perceive the world.

Based on all the above—and as I explained before—I decided to change my strategy. I went on another type of dating Web site where I knew there would be no more than ten or so contacts a day, not seventy guys clicking on my profile because I have long blond hair. Most of them just click on anything they think looks interesting all the time, and they don't even bother to read your profile.

The first date I went on came one-hour late, and I wish I hadn't waited. It was not worthwhile. The second one was not much better, looked nothing like his picture, and was a dud. The third one was an interesting guy. He was in music and sound and lived at the Sunshine Coast. He had lots of appeal, and I felt attracted to him. We had our second and third date, and we kissed.

Next day, I heard nothing. The day after—nothing. The agony of these things when you start thinking, *Was my breath off? Did I say something stupid? Was there another more interesting, better looking person than I?* All these questions…so I did the wrong thing, and I left him an FB message. He seemed standoffish in his reply, so I thought, *No, I have had enough of this.*

I had asked him, "Can I call you?"

He had replied, "Sure."

And then I did something different for the first time in my life. I thought I am valuable, and I deserve to be treated better than this. I did not call him. He had my number. If he really was interested in me, he could call me back. I made a date with the next one who came available on the dating Web site.

He spoke about spiritual books and the importance of forgiving, so I thought I will give this a go. And we went on our first date. It lasted eleven hours, and we talked and talked and talked some more. I made sure this time not to be eager or hurried, but to take my time and evaluate if this person was the right type of man for me—if we shared the same hierarchy of priorities and if we had a similar world-view. Was this someone I could share the rest of my life with? Regardless of the promise I made to myself on taking things slowly, we were engaged nine months later and married seventeen months after our first date.

We share a very interesting connection and can talk about anything that matters to us. We have up and down days like they have in every relationship, but we keep working on it. We always find each other in the beliefs we share. The first time we went on a holiday, we went to the Mouses Houses at Springbrook. This is a group of quaint little houses located in the rain forest. They are self-contained and have an open fire and outdoor Jacuzzi—all very romantic; we had the time of our lives. We had decided to make vision boards during that trip. I had made some before, and, to my experience, they really worked. I had made one with the things I was looking for in my partner, and Brad was 80 percent compliant with this wish list. Some words had faded due to water that had run over it, so some things were different, but the essence was the same. It was freakish how fast the vision boards became reality. The year after that, we decided to make one together. I am curious to see what will happen to that one and will keep you posted.

Another example of how a vision worked was a picture of a house on my office wall. I buy monthly tickets to try and win a house whilst supporting children's hospitals. The pictures of the house of that month really resonated with me. I had put it on my wall and looked at it whilst daydreaming how it would feel to live in a house like that.

I now live in that house. I did not win it, but I ended up renting it, realising later on after living there that it was the same prize house. So we did have a car, a dog, travel trips—you name it, my engagement ring, and so on. I experienced that the important thing is to put it out there; don't worry about the how and the when. Don't overthink—just feel the way you would feel when you already had everything on your vision board.

THINGS THAT MAKE MY DAY

I try to live my life as if my dreams were already my reality. I feel how I would feel if my dreams had already come true. When I lose track of how to do this, I would read the book *The Law of Attraction* (Esther and Jerry Hicks) again. They explain how to concentrate on being in the right vibrational energy so well.

I try to stay in the honeymoon phase and just feel the love inside my body all the time. I don't give up when I am having a down day or a day when things seem to go wrong. Every day is a reason to celebrate and get into that mood. From when you open your eyes, think this is going to be a wonderful day. Today, I will do nice things for myself, and I will be good to myself. I will enjoy life, and I will be happy. I make myself a nice cup of my favourite tea and sip it while I concentrate already on feeling how good the upcoming day will be. When stuck, I do some EFT and tap on the things that come up from my subconscious mind. I will often choose to wear clothes that make me feel vibrant, like my "happy" pants—they are so colourful that wearing them makes me happy. I also pay attention to how I feel in relation to what I choose to eat. Which choice of foods are making me feel better about myself and which ones make me feel tired after eating them. When my organism seems to be in a rut, I might do a ten-day lemon detox to get it all fine-tuned again. Because I so firmly believe in this detox, it works for me. I love to get rid of the toxins that build up in my system, and, more and more, I avoid building them up. I buy more organic food, eat unprocessed as much as possible, and have less and less sugar intake. I find that healthy eating habits make me feel more vibrant and not depleted afterwards.

Again, it is more important how you feel about what you eat than what you put in your mouth. What we believe and how we feel about the food we take in will help or obstruct with the processing of it. They tested the difference between French and American food, and the amount of fat, sugar, and carbs is very similar. Only, the French love their food and are convinced it is the best food in the world. They savour every bite and enjoy the eating process, whilst Americans have a tendency to eat it fast and feel guilty about eating their "fast" food. There are less obese people in France than in the US.

I also have an ongoing process of establishing daily health routines: starting off my day with some yoga, followed by walking my dog. I look for ways to move my body that I enjoy, and that make me feel good. I sometimes get off-track and then beat myself up over it; I noticed this does not work. It works best when I really have fun moving my body rather then sweat in a gym if I don't like the environment of a gym to begin with. I listen to my body talking to me and letting me know when I am on track, and I show it some respect.

I live close to the beach, so I love to take my dog for a walk there. It is an off-leash area, and he loves to run around and play with the other dogs. He is not afraid to go into the water, although sometimes it gets a bit rough, but he is careful. When we don't walk, we just sit a bit on our towel and look at the waves. The other day, there was a whale quite close to the beach. They are magical creatures and have a special energy around them. Everyone felt uplifted by their presence. I have been on a boat whale watching and was very close to them. They feel so alive and are so big that it is pure magic to be that close.

REPROGRAMMING

I realised, after ten years of unsuccessful dating, that I had commitment phobia. I used to think it was bad luck or negative karma following me around. I kept meeting these people who were not suitable for a relationship with me. I felt the fear of commitment the most on the weeks coming up to my wedding. I was not a spring chicken; I was getting married for the first time. I thought, *Is this really a good thing to do? Is this really necessary?* I came up with lots of excuses and reasons not to get married. I had so many limiting beliefs when it came to marriage! I was lucky enough to have a life coach, a colleague of my then fiancé, offered me some free sessions to work through them. We were saving money for the wedding, so I could not afford to pay for one, and he was very understanding. Malcolm Neal, from Fuel 4 Business, used NLP (neuro linguistic programming) to change my beliefs, and now I can't remember what I used to think. That is the strange thing about NLP. When properly done, you can become the kind of person you always dreamed of being. You only need to make sure that what you believe on a conscious and subconscious level is in harmony with who and what you want to be. I also had a good "why" I wanted the change. At that time in my life, I knew that the biggest lessons I needed to learn would be offered through an intimate personal relationship. I felt great by myself and did not contact the outer world when not in the mood. My life was a bit like the monk on top of a mountain—feeling great whilst meditating all day alone, but then he had to come down from the mountaintop and buy a lolly before he could self-realise, because he still had the hunger for it. He had to experience the feeling of what he was longing for before he could let go of it.

I got very interested in seeing how the brain can be reprogrammed and rewired. The plasticity of the brain is unique! There will be so many possibilities coming up in the future to heal people through rewiring the brain. I find this something to look forward to.

SOME OTHER THINGS I NOTICED

I think the need to look for new endeavours and obstacles to jump into, time and time again, comes from my early years. Repeatedly hearing, *"No, Nadine, this is not good enough! You can do so much better! You have to be better than you are now. Stop being so lazy,"* translated into two things for me:

1. I am not good enough and
2. I constantly have to prove myself and put the bar a bit higher.

Yes, I Do & I Did It

Furthermore, I can go from being hyperactive to having very quiet moments and even procrastination. All or nothing, like the Russian mountains. I got rather good at getting in the "zone" when the deadline is breathing down my neck. That is when I excel, with only little time left and lots of work that needs to be done fast. When I make a painting, it ripens for a long time inside me. Then one day, after I have relaxed completely, it will just pour out of me.

No matter how much I enjoy conquering new horizons, I also form many habits on my way. Some are habits that serve my well-being; others, not so much. I often have to catch my thoughts while working, so I don't fall back into old unhealthy habits. It is funny how it takes at least twenty-one days to build up a new healthy habit, but to take up an unhealthy one is often straight away.

Although smoking took a while before I started enjoying it, giving it up was probably one of the most difficult things I did in my life. I went cold turkey using willpower only and was very sick the first couple of days. Now, I can hardly imagine I used to smoke, and I find it weird that some people still do.

I read the story "The Last Smoker" (W.F. Hermans) as a teenager, and Hermans kind of knew, eventually, that people would not be able to smoke as they wished. I was also addicted to reading the works of Gerard Reve, Harry Mulish, Johan Daisne, Hugo Claus, and so on. My favourite Flemish author, whom I only really appreciated at an older age even though I liked him since I was a teenager, was Willem Elschot. He had that dry sense of humour and a combination of being funny and sad at the same time. Reading fast and reading a lot is one of those habits that take an effort to set aside for a while. I had to force myself to follow the request not to read during my writing retreats.

What I also noticed is that there is this whole generation of people who believed that "real art" can only be achieved through suffering. They believed that those who suffer can deliver better art than those who have never known any suffering. I do not know if that is true, because I think we all suffer at some level. We all share the basic guilt of our separation from the state of oneness with God. It might be deeply in the subconscious for most people, but when we look for it, we will find it. We believe we left God behind to create our own world and put the ego in charge to run the show. At a deeper level, we all know this. I used to fight it a lot, and I did because I was not interested in being one with everything. How boring is that? I wanted to be special, to be unique, and loved because of that.

Looking for love outside myself made me feel like a cat chasing her tail. I heard the other day that we are already the love we are seeking, and that we should stop chasing it. Love is already part of what we are. The only thing we need to do is recognise this and drop our guard and allow it.

ALLOW

The more I tried to belong in all the different phases in my life, the less I did. When I started giving up the need for approval, I started to experience more approval. I allowed more and more of the real me to shine through. I was open about the way I looked at the world through a spiritual lens. I become more true to the way I really was. Most of all, I started to accept myself the way I was. With self-acceptance, recognition arrived. I accepted I was good at my job, and my boss always encourages me. It is like extra cream in my soup. I no longer need the approval, so it is there showing up in my life. Many things start to happen in my life that allow me to spend more time doing things I enjoy, like writing. I still write mostly at night, so I have some more work to do before I can fully allow the creative me to take the overhand. I like to see myself as a work in progress—getting there one baby step at a time.

The things I used to do to seek recognition and approval make me laugh now. I would wear clothes that are very uncomfortable but "in." Of course, we all wear the high heels that are not really comfortable, but we keep wearing them because it makes us feel sexy, and it makes us feel as if we belong. We also wear pants that were so tight it took ten minutes to put them on, and so on. Why do we have the need to belong? Does this kind of behaviour come from the days we used to live in small communities, and that being an outsider was equal to limiting your chances of survival? Is that why I had the need for support? I decided that no matter what reason I had for this need for support, I would try to feel supported all the time. By the chair I am sitting on, the bed I am lying in, or the ground I walk on, I repeat to myself what Byron Katie says so beautifully: "We are either standing up, lying down, or sitting, and everything else is a story."

Who doesn't love a good story? Maybe we just can't get enough of making them up. We make up happy stories, sad stories, all kinds of stories, just to keep us entertained so we would forget about our guilt, our primary guilt. The story I believe is as follows:

We make up guilt stories and see a lot of things wrong outside of us instead of owning our guilt. We project our guilt onto the world and onto our own body. We hide in our made-up world and body, so God cannot reach us to punish us. We, for some stupid reason (tiny mad idea; it is called in ACIM), think that God or the "universal force of love" is after revenge, because we left the state of unity. Only the ego can come up with such a thought. A perfect oneness who is only love and who wants to punish doesn't make any sense at all. Yet to the ego is a great scapegoat.

Sometimes people say, "If there would be a God, there would not be all this misery in the world." I think that God does not see the misery. He still sees us as one; he sees the part that never left him, and not the other part that had a "tiny mad idea" that forgot its real power when it fell asleep. It is comparable to us seeing someone having a nightmare. We know they are having a bad dream, and that they are safe sleeping in their bed.

MONEY AND LOVE

I strongly held on to the belief that to make good money, you have to suffer in your job and work very hard, long hours. It is not possible to make good money the easy way, and certainly not by doing something you enjoy doing. I tried very hard to find the good stuff in my work and to make it as enjoyable as possible, but the only real reason I got work was to make money to stay independent. The few times I tried something different, I failed and lost all the money I had worked very hard for. I had no idea why I couldn't be successful with what I liked doing. I did not see the connection in those days between my limiting beliefs and my daily reality.

I also had limiting beliefs about love. I was convinced that to be in a relationship, I had to hide who I really was, because I was unlovable. So, like a chameleon, I would change into that which the man of my desire was looking for, and then I claimed he did not love me because he did not know who I truly was. He only knew the fake me.

I had this obsession about earning lots of money for myself. Prove to myself that I was worth a lot of money. Prove that I was lovable because, in my mind, money and love were very mixed up and, in a way, similar. Venus, the planet of love, is also the planet of money, but I never understood that it is because both are energy. Money is energy, and it has different ways of showing up. Sometimes it shows up as a number in a computer somewhere, or numbers written on a piece of paper with a signature. Money is becoming less and less something we can touch—like gold coins—and more and more as something we can experience, like an energy or numbers in a computer. I no longer handle cash money on a daily basis. A week can go by without me touching dollars. I pay mostly with my cards, PayPal, or bank transfer, and I have also stopped issuing cheques. I like to have money in my wallet, though, because if I have a wad of fifty dollars in my wallet, I feel abundant. I think of all the things I could buy with it, and I don't even have to spend the dollars to feel the benefit of it. During the ten years I was single and making a good living, I had also convinced myself that since I was lucky with money, I had to experience bad luck with love. It was a situation of either or—both could not exist together.

FEELINGS

Most of what we really want in life is not something we can touch. It is a feeling that we are after. I am after the feeling of full bliss, abundance, magnificence, powerfulness, and of being energized, not the material things I think I need to supply me these feelings. Another misconception: "Money makes you happy." No, "happy" makes you happy. Like attracts like. If I feel happy, I feel wealthy and rich. I can have wealth, and it would be worthless unless I felt it. It is all in our perception. The way I feel about things is how I experience things. I noticed more and more that I experience what I think. Every thought is projected outside of us and seen as separate, therefore I like to own my thoughts and my projections. I never see others at fault; I only try to see my story behind whatever happens. It is not an easy exercise to let life happen and to just be. I always want to interfere and get stuff right. *It has to be this way. No, that way is better, and I can do that even better.* Constantly seeking, constantly looking for something outside myself and forgetting the treasure inside. I was like that beggar who sat for years begging on a wooden crate full of gold. I can see very clearly how I spent all those first years exactly like that. Always on the run, on the move, and blaming everyone else for my unhappiness. I forgot so often to make room for contemplation, to just sit still and let it all be: to allow. Now, I still have to remind myself to do it on a regular basis. Luckily, my body gives me clear signals when I forget. That is the big advantage of being in a body; it gives clues where we are offtrack.

THE BODY

We spend billions of dollars on medications and relevant research, but we hardly spend any on research of the effects of stress on the body. If we could nail down how to avoid stress, there would be many more healthy people. Some diseases would probably disappear. There would no longer be any need for medicines. However, we concentrate on disease and not on health.

This is the reason I do not like campaigns that raise awareness for a disease. So many of them are pointing out how many ways anybody can get sick. The scary effect is feeding the mind with more fear than is already present. I would like our minds to be fed with good things—about health, about living life to the fullest, and about being happy just the way we are. Make people feel good about themselves and teach them how to love themselves. If you want to know more about this, I suggest you read *Dying To Be Me* by Anita Moorjani. She explains in a magnificent way how she clinically died and came back with the wisdom of how to be herself, to be happy, and how to concentrate on being healthy, not sickly.

Some people are still not convinced that our mind influences our body, like the medical doctor the other day whom I interviewed to see if she would be suitable as my GP. She couldn't see how our mind affects our body at all. She kept repeating, "I am medically trained," and got quite upset in the end. I did not choose her as my doctor. Instead, I will keep on looking for someone who does have a holistic approach and knows that placebos often work just as good or better than traditional medicines. It took me a lot of courage to decide that I would keep interviewing doctors until I found one I liked. It seemed very pretentious and unlike me to do this kind of research, but I have changed, and I now believe that my body deserves a doctor who understands the way I see how the mind affects the body.

I read Louise Hay in the late eighties, and then forgot about it for a while. Over the last ten years, her blue book has been a constant companion. As soon as I find something wrong in my body, I look it up. Asthma, allergies, sore throat, legs, arms—all is so clearly explained. It is so basic and simple that our left-brain will say, *"No, that is not possible. That would mean everyone is the same."* In a way, we are all made from the same universal energy material. We all have that piece of God in us, but we want to be different to stand out. It would be the death of the ego to be one with all that is, and that is a bit scary. The ego wants to live just like everyone else, and it needs negativity to feed upon. If we are too happy, the ego will find a way to make it more difficult for us to see if we can still be that happy in the face of adversity.

Then again, happiness only exists in this world. Anything that has an opposite is from this world. I have found nothing in the world that has no opposite. One thing exists in contrast to the other, dichotomy at his best. Luckily, we have sinners, or we would not know what a saint is. Luckily, we have bad, so we can experience the opposite. It goes on and on and on, until we come home again—when we no longer feel the need to "create" our own world. To realise the power of the mind is enormous, and it feels much safer to keep that at a distance.

Once you start playing around by consciously attracting that in your life—which you really want, instead of waiting to see what your subconscious will show you from the mind of a five-year-old—it gets interesting. The reason I say "a five-year-old" is because most of our beliefs, limiting and nonlimiting, are formed by that time. By the age of five, we have adopted the beliefs of our surroundings and have fully accepted the paradigm of the people who surround us. For the rest of our lives, we keep most of those paradigms, and we have very deep settled beliefs that we will carry with us for the next seventy, eighty, or whatever years we will pass in that lifetime. I only realised lately that I still make lots of my decisions based on what my five-year-old self believed without being aware of who or what was making the decision. If as a five-year-old I experienced that life was difficult and I heard my mother repeating often that "life was not even worth living," I believed *that*, and, because of the power of my mind, I projected *that* outside myself. I created a reality for me that was difficult, a life full of hindrances that were in alignment with my thoughts, or, should I say, my mother's thoughts that I had adopted at a very young age. This can go on for generations until someone breaks the chains and changes his or her core belief. This would be a person who starts digging into his or her subconscious to become aware of the thoughts that are no longer serving his or her emotions.

The biggest change I did last year was correcting my eyesight. After buying the EFT bundle, The Tapping World Summit (Nick Ortner), I decided to work on my eyes. Nick explains the EFT very clearly, and he had engaged several people, each specialised in a certain field, to have a one-hour session. Eleanore Duyndam had a special—"How to Improve Your Eyesight" with EFT, and I did it over and over again. I used to have minus 2, but after a couple of months, when I went to have my eyes checked, it was minus 1.75. The optometrist was very sceptical when I called her, and she said that I wanted to have my prescription changed to a lesser strength. When she saw that the test proved what I already told her, she was very amazed. Never had she seen a customer whose eyes got better in time. I told her about the tapping and how it had influenced my body in a way that can be measured. I told her I want to keep going until I no longer need any prescription. This is an ongoing process, but I will keep working on it. I am somehow convinced that is my fear of the future—creating short-sightedness. I can only see clearly what is here and now straight in front of me, but everything in the distance is kind of vague and misty.

THE MIND

I started training my mind when I realised that the untrained mind behaves like a bunch of wild horses all going in different directions. I am now trying to line them up to go in the same direction. The path I wanted my horses to go is the one I came from before becoming "human"—the experience of oneness with all that is.

The first thing I noticed was that I didn't know why my mind kept running around and why it can get so afraid of allowing things. Where does the need for control come from? Why do we want to be in control? Does it give us a feeling of safety or security? You may be having thoughts like: "Yeah, I can handle this"; "Leave it up to me. I am of logical mind. I can solve any problem"; "With me you are safe." To give up the need to have the logical mind control your life and to realign it with your feelings is scary. To control my wild horses meant to giving them free rein and trusting my instincts. Feel the horses and communicate with them with pictures and feelings. Know that when your heart is guiding them, they will follow. It's like when you're trying to jump over an obstacle with a real horse. First, you should throw your heart over the jump and look at the point were you want to be. Then you should allow the horse to follow that and give him the space to move freely, performing the jump elegantly, naturally.

It took years and years of practice, and I am not quite there yet. I still often like to be in charge, to be the boss. I don't like surprises, especially not negative ones. I was also convinced that as long as my logical mind is in charge, my body could not be harmed. Meanwhile, my stressful thoughts were creating havoc all over my body. Now, I changed that belief. The mind, especially the untrained mind, can be a danger for good health. It can create the right environment for all kinds of diseases to fester.

To realise how unlimited the mind is, how strong the subconscious influence in our life is, and, at the same time, realise that the conscience mind is not anywhere as strong an influencer is scary. It means that having only some positive thoughts on a conscious level is not going to do the trick. We will have to dig deeper into our subconscious mind and go to the source, the root, if we want to change the outcome. I spend a lot of time looking at what would come up from my subconscious mind and figuring out where my "beliefs" came from. When something negative happens—or should I say, something I judge negatively—I would immediately think, *Is that true? And is the opposite not just as true? When was the first time I had that belief? Is it my belief, or did I just take it from my parents, friends, and my environment?*

I just want to know what drives me, what makes me think I really am, and what concept of who I am keeps changing.

During the writing process of this book, I experienced the allowing at a very deep level. At times, I had no idea what I was doing, and that felt perfect. I was allowing the book to come through me. I wrote: "I am writing this book, and the universal force is flowing through me and giving me full support. It is directing me in all I need to say and write, and I can step aside."

CHANGE AND TIME

Another typical thing in this world I experienced is change. Everything is constantly changing; there is nothing permanent. Everything is constantly moving like energy. The energy is directed by the subconscious into forms. In a way, it is what we believe that gives form. We experience that certain forms are good and others are bad, and it reinforces certain beliefs. To experience real change in my life, I do not need to change continents. I discovered that the only thing that brought change in my life was changing my paradigm. I needed to change the way I thought the universe was structured and how it was operating. By creating new belief systems, positive ones, on a conscious and subconscious level, the world of form was influenced in a positive way. Like in quantum physics, the result of an experiment depends on the observer, what an observer thinks is predominant for the result of an experiment. Without an observer, there is nothing. When there is no one in the forest to hear a tree fall, there is no noise. Someone needs to be there to receive it for it to exist. The movie *What the Bleep Do We Know!?* was a confirmation of many things I had seen and experienced. It made me see that I was not alone in experiencing certain facts in my life. It inspired me to even more consciously try and create the experiences I really wanted.

One of the things I experience every day is time. Time has always been an amazing concept to me. Does it or doesn't it exist? Is it part of our projection and the "creation" of the ego, so that it has a context to work in? Although we can measure it, the experience of time is very subjective. Waiting can last so much longer than doing something we enjoy. We can lose the sense of time, but it could still be measured. Is it linear, or is it all happening now at the same moment? Is it a context we created in the dream to have a parameter to measure our evolution? We can't really grasp this, because whenever we look at the time, it is always now. It never is the future or the past. Those two concepts only exist in my mind. I can see how something happened in the past, and when I am telling or thinking about it, I am doing that in the now. The same applies for future thoughts. I do not have them in the future; I have them here and now. I can read over and over *The Power of Now* by Eckhart Tolle, and each time see new things. He has mastered that subject of time and how only the now exists perfectly.

With time and change comes the aging process. Aging seems to have changed, and people of fifty are now like forty-year-olds used to be in those days. Is it due to plastic surgery, different habits, or more health consciousness? Or has our whole consciousness just risen with the human race? We all live much longer and look ten or twenty years younger than the previous generation.

Maybe we are starting to realise that age is just a number, and that we are only as old as we feel. The more people adjust their old beliefs to these new ones, the more the reality will change. With reality, I actually mean the reality in this dream. Because it is a dream, we can change things and manifest them differently. The power of the mind is getting more and more recognised, and, hopefully, will turn into a recognised science one day.

Nadine Nelen

CHANGING

I had to do much more than just positive thinking to get real change. I had to change the way I feel. The emotions are running my world. If I am in the right state of mind, the right kinds of things happen to me. If I am happy, I attract joyful experiences in my world. If I am sad and angry, I attract more of that in my world. Now, how do I stay in the joyful state of mind? By doing things that bring me joy. In the morning, I try to concentrate in doing what will make me happy right now. Will it be a sleep in? My yoga? A walk on the beach? A chat with a good friend? Then I aim for it.

Even if in the beginning, it is only some small stuff that I will afford myself; but it will grow organically like a plant that I water and nourish every day. Every day, I water my self-esteem and the idea that it is okay for me to do the things that make me feel happy and good about myself. Sometimes I just buy something for someone else to make them feel good. Paying a cup of coffee forward, giving a present, or any act of random kindness can make me feel good for days. Little by little, it became a new way of existing for me and of having fun going through my life. I attracted more of that which I was concentrating on.

The trick is to catch the mind before it falls too deep in the downward spiral. Sometimes one little remark you get can trigger a lot of deeply buried negative thoughts that you hadn't come around yet to change. Whenever people upset me, I feel very grateful and thank them profusely. They are helping me out in a big way by pointing out where I still have some work to do. They are helping me pave my way to happiness. Until nothing upsets me in this world, I have work to do.

There will be thoughts to look at and see if they are still serving me or if I would rather let them go. If it is not other people who point you towards the areas in your life where you can work upon, then it will be the body. Any ailment I ever found in my body has always pointed me to an ailment in my thinking. I look everything up in Louise Hay's blue book and make sure I understand the way my body is communicating with me. I want to use it for the purpose it has. When I do have something giving me pain or trouble, I find it very difficult to allow it and to love its presence, to accept the "isness" of the things and just be the space for it. Be the space where things happen without judging them and labelling them as good or bad.

I often start by first letting out the raw emotion. If it is anger, I go and beat a pillow very hard and scream until I feel that the anger has left my body. Then I sit down on my mediation pillow, have some incense burning, and turn my mind inside. I just sit and breathe in and out, in and out, and let the thoughts run on the screen inside my head without clinging to them, just having them run past. Then I connect to the highest force I can reach and have it run through me. Feeling the peace that it will bring. Feeling the aliveness inside me. Knowing I am alive. Then I start having positive affirmation going through my mind and often use EFT while I do my self-talk. I tap on my body while I say my affirmations. Even if negative thoughts slip in, I just keep tapping on them. Then when I feel really good, I go and shower the negative emotion off me, and, at the end, I imagine beautiful light coming out of the shower head—instead of water—and being filled with the most pure energy. Then I am ready to face the world and to be a happy partaker in whatever life will bring to me.

During the day, I sometimes need to adjust. Other things will pop up to test how deep I did my clearing of negative beliefs. It will soon be clear how much has been solved. The more we interact with others, the more we realise how much more we need to do. They say, "If you think you are enlightened, go and spend a weekend with your parents."

Some days I work from home, and I hardly get to see anyone; I feel very peaceful. Then the weekend comes, and I try to find a parking spot to buy my groceries, but someone takes the spot I had been waiting for straight before my nose. This is a very good example that tests my level of acceptance of what is…or people jumping the cue I am "patiently" lining up in. More and more I try to see all this as opportunities to grow and not as negative things happening to me.

There are so many opportunities for growth, for learning more about yourself, and what makes you tick—to learn what it is that makes you "you" and not someone else. What are your trigger points? Is it being ignored? Taken for granted? Being bullied? Others telling you that you don't know how to do certain things that they know better? Being hurt by negativity? Not being accepted, valued? The list goes on and on and on.

Remember, each time you catch yourself making a negative statement in your mind that is upsetting, have it follow with the question, "Is it true, and can I absolutely know that it is true?" Then see how the opposite thought is just as true. Remember, we are in duality and the opposite exists and is evenly true. We have the yin and yang inside us. As long as we can keep a balance and accept the way things are, we will strive and feel better about ourselves.

There is a procession in Belgium, in the city of Echternach, and it goes on for ages because they do three steps forward and two steps back. That is how I see spiritual development. We take three steps forward, and then when we have a test, we go two steps back. Good thing is, we are still advancing into self-realisation and to more understanding of the fact that we are spiritual beings having a human experience, not the other way around.

We also see more and more people around us with similar experiences, and they write and talk about new paradigms. It is becoming more normal to say these days in a normal conversation: "This is something I experienced in several of my past lives." Thirty years ago, no one said anything like that. There was only one life in those days. Maybe the consciousness of the whole planet is rising, and that is good news. People become less violent and self-centred when they realise we are all connected and come from the same energy.

We can share then the abundance that already exists on this earth.

BALANCE

We work hard and long hours, and our heart is sometimes saying, *"Please don't; you are putting too much stress on me,"* but we don't listen. *The heart is just a muscle; it should obey. I am in control, not my body—mind over body.*

"Mens sana in corpore sano" says clearly that there needs to be a balance between the health of the mind and the body, and—I think—especially between the subconscious mind and the body. We function at our best when we are in balance, when we align the poles of the dichotomy and have them dancing together in harmony. Yin and yang performing a blissful eternal dance, letting it flow and dance, the two faces showing and both being just as important to each other to make sure it doesn't tip over.

I like the saying: "Life can only be understood backwards; but it must be lived forwards." So true. The biggest disasters in life often turn out to be the biggest blessings in disguise. We learn and grow so much from those moments that life would not be worthwhile without them. Each time I lost everything and had to start from scratch again, I ended up in a much better space than where I was before. When I lost the first apartment I ever bought, I ended up in a house with horse stables in the backyard. When I lost a job I loved,

I ended up with a job that was ten times better and more suited for me, allowing me to work from home. When a relationship ended, each time, no matter how sad I was afterwards, I could always see that it was for the better. Sometimes I look back at relationships I tried and can't see what I was trying to prove with it. They seem so unlike me, or the "me" I have now become. It's like I look back into someone else's life instead of my own and try to understand what she ever saw in the person involved. When I was in pain over my loss, I always turned inside, safely into my inner sanctuary, and tried to see the lesson I had signed up for. Who did I need to forgive and why? Where was I holding back on my full potential? Where was I giving away my own power? Every time it hurt, it felt like a crack was showing up in my armour. Funny writing the word "armour"; I noticed how it is so close to "amour" ("love" in French). I had to learn to love and forgive myself and others. When I lost my first business and the first apartment at the same time, I did feel liberated as well. I suddenly no longer felt weighted down with the things I associated with; I could reinvent myself again. I could finally take time to start those art classes again, to go and ride my horse more often, to get a dog, and to design the house I really wanted. I screamed when I lost the first "drafts" of what I thought I should have and be, but then I settled down to allow the universe to give me what was more in line with my emotional state, feelings, and awareness at that specific moment. When I lost that job I loved so much, I had a chance to start my own company again and to express my creative side that eventually led me to start writing this book.

The cleansing of losing is enormous and gives a great advantage. Loss can be felt as something cracking inside ourselves. Where there is a crack, there is space for more light to shine in.

To align myself with the universe and to see that all is good in my world and exactly the way it is supposed to be, I sometimes use the following exercise from Louise Hay: Take a mirror. Look yourself in the eyes and say: "I love you".

I love and approve of myself is one of the most difficult things I find to say in the mirror, and during the tapping exercises. I am so much more comfortable hitting myself over the head with criticism than I am with praise. I seem to think it is dirty to praise myself, almost like masturbating, which—we were taught at a very young age—was unhealthy and could make you blind. It made you impure at the least, and God would know and would punish you. We feel praising ourselves is often a case of vanity, and we do not want to be vain. That is the last thing on earth we want to be seen as. I can love myself without vanity and stay humble apparently. I haven't figured that one out completely yet, but stay tuned, I am planning to work it out and write a book about it.

THE END

Writing about the past has brought me back in the state of mind I was in during those days. Like an actor who identifies with his role so much that he becomes the role. I identified with my past "me." The "me" I no longer am, as I have changed a lot of core beliefs. It is very similar to regression, where you live through it all again.

One of the things I realised when I read the book after writing it is that a common theme in many of my relationship issues was "lying." Only now when I am writing it down do I suddenly realise this: was life trying to tell me that I was the one who was lying? I was not living my own truth. I was living by the truth of other people! I was trying to fit in a shoe size and model that was not going to get me to the ball I wanted to go. One day at a time, I now try to live by what sounds true to me and what I think will serve me well. Happiness being my main goal now, I am no longer afraid of the consequences of my choices.

I can now recommend to anyone looking to release old beliefs that no longer serve him or her to write a book. It is a big cleansing process, and it has realigned me with my life purpose.

Thank you, Tom Bird for your wise words that help me give birth to this book and making it all happen.

Acknowledgments

Thank you to anyone who has ever crossed my path, you were all meaningful. Most of all I want to thank "the unseen" the force that cannot be seen with the physical eyes but that has been instrumental to put it all on paper. Without the muse there would be no book, only a story.

Thank you to Tom Bird and Rama for helping me giving birth to my "firstborn" book. Thank you to Marilyn Mckinley and Jim Hill for your free and sound advise and corrections and last but not least to my husband, Brad Alder.

www.ingramcontent.com/pod-product-compliance
Lightning Source LLC
Chambersburg PA
CBHW022216090526
44584CB00012BB/787